*O*n 10th September 1992, Their Majesties King Juan Carlos and Queen Sofía inaugurated the Permanent Collection of the Museo Nacional Centro de Arte Reina Sofía, *which hitherto had housed temporary exhibitions only. From then on the* Centro *was to be a true Museum possessing, extending and exhibiting its own holdings.*

However, the origin of the building which houses the MNCARS dates far back in time. After a number of vicissitudes, in the second half of the 18th century it was decided that the architect Francisco Sabatini should be commissioned to design a new hospital. Sabatini, however, was not able to complete the building and only part of the original plans were executed. Since then and virtually up to the present day, various alterations and additions have been made to the Hospital. Despite demands that the building be demolished, it has managed to survive and through a Royal Decree of 1977 was declared a "Historical Artistic Monument".

In 1980, work began on the restoration of the hospital under Antonio Fernández Alba and at the end of 1988 José Luis Iñíguez de Onzoño and Antonio Vázquez de Castro made the final alterations, among which the three steel and glass lift towers, designed in collaboration with the British architect Ian Ritchie, are of special importance.

Two years before, in 1986, certain areas of the Museum, which was still known as the Centro de Arte Reina Sofía, *were inaugurated for temporary activities. The museum was directed by Carmen Giménez in her capacity as head of the* Centro Nacional de Exposiciones *("National Centre for Exhibitions"), dependent on the Ministry of Culture.*

Shortly after, in 1988, the Centro *became a* Museo Nacional *("National Museum"), by Royal Decree replacing the old* Museo Español de Arte Contemporáneo *(*MEAC, "Spanish Museum of Contemporary Art"*). Tomás Llorens was the first Director of the institution from June 1988 to December 1990.*

The Garden.

On 28th December 1990, María de Corral was appointed as Director of the Museum.

In September 1994, José Guirao Cabrera was appointed as the new Director.

The Royal Decree of 27th May 1988, through which the Centro de Arte Reina Sofía *became a* Museo Nacional, *specified that the Museum's holdings should consist of works from two sources: the collections belonging to the old MEAC, and acquisitions made by the MNCARS itself. Furthermore, the possibility of transferring the 20th-century holdings housed in the Prado Museum, especially those connected with Pablo Picasso's* Guernica, *had been considered since 1988. The transfer was authorised on 17th March 1995 through Royal Decree 410/1995, which dealt with the reorganisation of the holdings of the* Museo Nacional del Prado *and the* Museo Nacional Centro de Arte Reina Sofía.

Also among the MNCARS holdings are legacies made to the Centro, *one of the most important being the fifty-six works left to the Museum by Salvador Dalí, the "Painter of Cadaqués", in his will in 1982.*

Room 6. Pablo Picasso

In the case of the works of Joan Miró in the Museum's collection,
most of these came into its possession as a result of the first
enforcement of the "Spanish Historical Heritage Act" (which
concerns the payment of death duties) implemented in 1985.
The internal organisation of the MNCARS is as follows:

– Director's Office
– Art Management
– General Management
– Collections Department
– Restoration Department
– Registrar's Office
– Exhibitions Department
– Audiovisual Department
– Communications Department
– Library and Archive

The Permanent Collection occupies Floors Two and Four.
Floor Two contains works showing the development of 20th-
century art from the beginning of the century until the

Room 7. Joan Miró

Spanish Civil War (1936-39). Two rooms for temporary
exhibitions enable the Museum to show holdings which are
rarely seen in the Permanent Collection. Floor Four covers the
development of art between the end of the Civil War and the
present day. The exhibition ends in rooms with temporary
exhibitions featuring the most recent artistic manifestations.
For the Permanent Collection four fundamental and
complementary criteria have been taken into account.
Time: giving a chronological view of the Spanish art and
artists of the 20th century. These works are compared with
others by international artists, especially those who have links
with the arts in Spain.
Theme: which has been taken as the basis for connecting
the successive art movements in Spain during the period covered.
Assessment: by which an attempt has been made to highlight
the special nature of individual contributions and their
relationship to group movements and tendencies.
Space: which has made it possible to dedicate Floor Four to the
Permanent Collection, where until now only temporary

Room 35. Antoni Tàpies

exhibitions were held. In this way the Collection is divided into two parts on two different levels – Floors Two and Four – thus underlining the difference between the contents of both, with the avant-garde movements of the past on Floor Two and contemporary works on Floor Four.
The layout of the MNCARS is as follows:

- *Floor 0: Photographic laboratory, storage, workshops, restaurant and loading bay.*
- *Floor One: Vestibule, coffee shop, bookshop, auditorium, convention room, press room, temporary exhibitions room.*
- *Floor Two: Permanent collection.*
- *Floor Three: Library, documentation centre, recordings, drawings and photographs, and temporary exhibition rooms.*
- *Floor Four: Permanent collection. Restoration Department.*
- *Floor Five: Offices.*

Some of the works from the Permanent Collection may be substituted by others not included in this guide when they are out on temporary loan to other exhibitions.

The room in which the Permanent Collection begins contains a selection of those names and tendencies from the Spanish art scene at the beginning of this century which were the immediate predecessors of the avant-garde. At the end of the 19th century and the beginning of the 20th, there were two main centres of artistic activity in Spain: Catalonia and the Basque Country. Within the framework of Catalan Modernisme *are artists such as Ramón Casas, the great portraitist who, with great severity of composition and soberness of colour, depicted the social and political events of his time. Together with Casas's works are other original ones by the landscape artists Santiago Rusiñol and Joaquín Mir. The paintings of Darío de Regoyos, who associated with the Catalonian scene, depict open spaces with a Divisionist technique.*

Francisco Iturrino, Juan de Echevarría and Ignacio Zuloaga were artists linked to the Basque scene who won international recognition at the beginning of the century. Iturrino was the only Spanish painter to fully exploit the aesthetic precepts of Fauvism.

Noucentisme, *a tendency supported by Eugenio D'Ors, appeared as a reaction to* Modernisme. *D'Ors advocated a new form of artistic and literary classicism. The works of Isidro Nonell, which are usually considered as belonging to this tendency, nevertheless elude conventional classification. Concerned with depicting the lowest social classes, he accentuated monumentality and eliminated the anecdotal.*

The works of three sculptors – José Clara, Julio Antonio, and Mateo Inurria – demonstrate the diversity of directions to which Noucentista *classicism gave rise. The painter Hermenegildo Anglada Camarasa, however, shunned this* Noucentista *trend and developed his own personal iconography within* Modernisme *and Symbolism.*

ANGLADA CAMARASA

Hermenegildo Anglada Camarasa

Born in Barcelona in 1871, he died in Pollensa in 1959. In the closing years of the 19th century he settled in the French capital, where he discovered the Paris night life that was to be one of his favourite themes during his early period. After successful exhibitions in Belgium, Germany, England, Italy and France, he settled in Pollensa just as War World I broke out. His painting, which began with naturalist style landscapes, developed gradually until he finally turned to working with large canvases, mainly painting female portraits of Modernista *inspiration and with bright colours.*

1

Hermenegildo Anglada-Camarasa
Retrato de Sonia de Klamery,
Condesa de Pradère, c. 1913
(Portrait of Sonia de Klamery,
Countess Pradère)
Oil on canvas
187 x 200 cm
Reg. n° 00629

Anglada Camarasa's early works are identified with the *Modernisme* then in fashion in his native Catalonia. After 1907, he painted night life in cabaret scenes filled with translucent and opalescent women, whom he raised to the level of veritable living jewels.

In 1909, Diaghilev's *Ballet Russe* came to Paris, with Nijinsky and Pavlova as its leading dancers. This was a social and artistic event that was to revolutionise tastes and customs. The sets and costumes with their vivid oranges, fuchsias and greens were to make so deep an impression on Anglada that from then on the pale tones of his female portraits gave way to multicoloured brilliance.

Alexandre Cirici said with reference to this: "The *Portrait of Sonia de Klamery*, lying on a branch, covered in Chinese embroidery, surrounded by birds of paradise, illustrates a theatrical world of fantasy that was a kind of translation of Russian folklore into Spanish terms, into a brilliant, worldly game at a time when Anglada was a commercial success and was surrounded by the Court of Argentineans in Paris."

Isidro Nonell

Born in Barcelona in 1873, where he also died in 1911. In 1896, he produced a series of paintings and drawings depicting the deformed and mentally retarded which he subsequently exhibited, receiving unfavourable reviews from the critics due to the crude reality of the theme. After a period in which he frequented the Els Quatre Gats *in Barcelona, he travelled to Paris in 1899 and settled in the Montmartre area, associating with the avant-garde art circles. He subsequently returned to Barcelona, where he lived out the rest of his life and produced his most interesting works, whose themes always dealt with marginalization and squalor.*

2

Isidro Nonell
***Niebit*,1909**
Oil on canvas
130 x 88 cm
Reg. n° 01197

The early work of Isidro Nonell, which concentrated on the poorer classes of the Barcelona of the times – particularly on gypsy women – proved incomprehensible not only to the art critics but even to his models, who could not recognize themselves amid Nonell's images of poverty and misery. From the time of his 1910 exhibition at the *Faianç Català* Galleries in Barcelona, Nonell's iconography underwent a considerable change, although the process had in fact been taking place during the three or four years prior to the exhibition. His original blue and green tones gave way to ochres and pinks, as can be seen in the range of colours in the canvas *Niebit* ("Niebit"). However, this picture still contains features typical of his previous period, such as the absorbed attitude of the figure, and the choice of model – yet another gypsy girl. This "ethnic peculiarity" of Nonell's gradually disappeared between this time and his death in 1911.

*N*ext to the room devoted to the first avant-garde movements, although completely independent of it, is the room dedicated to José Gutiérrez Solana, one of Spain's most original artists and the creator of a form of Expressionism all his own.

In spite of the noteworthy originality of his works, his way of working lay in deeply traditional Spanish origins – Valdés Leal, Ribera, Goya, Zurbarán, even El Greco and the early work of Velázquez – although there is one non–Spanish exception – Brueghel the Elder.

Highly-defined outlines edging the motifs and powerful brush-strokes distributing the colour are outstanding features of his technique. Both of these – the outline and the colour field – produced dramatic scenes of a sturdy compositional structure.

In Solana's later years – a period which spanned the 20s – his canvases were usually large in size, thus contributing to the increased monumentality of the characters portrayed on them. Colour was applied with greater harmony and more richly than in his early paintings and, in general, his palette was lighter and more highly perfected.

Among Solana's subjects, three are particularly evident: those related to the people, streets and popular fiestas of Madrid; those depicting the habits and customs of the España Negra ("Dark Spain"); and the portraits.

3

José Gutiérrez Solana
La tertulia del Café de Pombo, 1920
(The Gathering at the Café de Pombo)
Oil on canvas
162 x 211.5 cm
Reg. n° 00915

An emblematic painting among Solana's works, it also
reveals his fondness for the gatherings of intellectuals which
were so common during the first thirty years of this century.
They took place in the most famous cafés of Madrid, such
as the *Nuevo Levante* in Calle Arenal, the *Universal*, the
Candelas, and above all, in the one whose name is the title
of this picture, the *Pombo*.
Donated to the Spanish State by Ramón Gómez de la
Serna in 1947, it had already been exhibited in the *Salón de
Otoño* in Madrid before becoming the property of the
Museo de Arte Contemporáneo. This *Salón* was held in
1920 at the famous Madrid café whose name the painting
takes.
Grouped around Ramón Gómez de la Serna, who appears
in the centre of the composition, are personalities from the
worlds of art and letters of the times: Manuel Abril, Tomás
Borrás, José Bergamín, José Cabrero, Mauricio Bacarisse,
Pedro Emilio Coll, Salvador Bartolozzi and Solana himself in
a magnificent self-portrait.

SOLANA

José Gutiérrez Solana

Born in Madrid in 1886, he died there in 1945. A devotee of the café gatherings in the capital, he attended several, such as those at the Café de Levante *and the* Café de Pombo, *immortalising the latter in one of his most important canvases. Not only a painter, he was also the author of various literary works, one being* Madrid. Escenas y costumbres *("Madrid. Scenes and Customs"), published in 1913. His style, which was closely linked to Expressionism, was directly inspired by the works of the Spanish painters of the Golden Age. To a certain extent, his aesthetics were associated with the pathetic view of the Spain of his times shared by the members of the* Generation of '98.

José Gutiérrez Solana
La procesión de la muerte, 1930
(The Procession of Death)
Oil on canvas
209 x 123 cm
Reg. n° 00871

The "macabre" Solana, fatally attracted to death and its irreversible effects, is best represented in this canvas, which became part of the State collection in 1945.
Here the painter paid tribute to a certain Hispanic tradition no less macabre than his own works and embodied in Valdés Leal's *Vanitas*. The imposing Baroque compositions, whose main aim was to remind the beholder of the fleetingness of time – *tempus fugit* – and the certainty of death, were revived in scenes such as this one as well as in other, very similar, ones like *La guerra* ("War", 1920), *El espejo de la muerte* ("The Mirror of Death", c. 1929), and *El osario* ("The Ossuary", 1931).
The attraction which this type of composition held for the artist is evident in his own stories about a morbid encounter at the *Museo de Escultura* in Valladolid. Thus, in his book *España Negra*, he described in great detail how he felt when, during his visit to the museum, he came face to face with a horrific skeleton (by the sculptor Gaspar Becerra), among whose bare bones wriggled a multitude of worms.

*T*he starting point of the international avant-garde lay in Cubism with Paris as one of its centres. Although some of the leading figures were Spanish artists like Picasso and Juan Gris, the avant-garde movements were not heard of in Spain until World War I, when artists, such as Sonia and Robert Delaunay, Francis Picabia and Rafael Barradas visited the peninsula.

The development from Noucentista classicism to a form of painting which, concerned with depicting the dynamism of the modern city, fell back on the resources of Cubism and Futurism, is evident in the works of the Uruguayan Joaquín Torres García. Furthermore, the works of Rafael Barradas, also from Uruguay and the founder of a tendency known as "Vibrationism", have many features in common with those of Torres García, who was a member of the Paris Abstraction-Création group and published his views on Universalismo constructivo ("Constructive Universalism") in 1941. Sonia and Robert Delaunay and Francis Picabia visited Spain during World War I. The Delaunays were associated with two avant-garde tendencies: "Simultaneism" and Orphism. Picabia's work developed from Cubism into a form of enigmatic painting preoccupied with machines and mechanisms and almost always provocative in its sexual symbology.

Jacques Lipchitz and Henri Laurens are examples of the range and limitations of Cubist sculpture. In some of his works, the former mixed elements of Cubism with features of primitive totemism. Laurens progressively turned Cubist analysis to a form of figurative art which brought together classicism and primitivism.

María Blanchard, a great friend of Juan Gris's and a faithful follower of his aesthetic principles, accepted and even encouraged Cubism as a new form of classicism, a concept championed by Josep María Junoy and Eugenio D'Ors.

5

Sonia Delaunay
Dubonnet, 1914
Watersoluble paint on canvas
61 x 76 cm
Reg. n° 12032

In 1912, Robert Delaunay painted his first non-objective picture, entitled *Disk*. In this circular oil painting, the artist divided the surface up into four sectors which, in turn, were made up of seven arcs with circumferences of different colours laid out according to the law of simultaneous contrast. Sonia applied the same ideas to her pictures that same year and, furthermore, also used the technique in textile and graphic design. The following year, in collaboration with the poet Blaise Cendrars, she illustrated the first book on "Simultaneism", entitled *La prose du Transsibérien*. With this book as her basis, in 1914, and just before her trip to Spain, she put her style of graphic design into practice in a number of advertising posters she had been commissioned to design. Cendrars called these "The greatest expression of our time."

In these posters, the arcs and coloured areas form a single space with the letters of the text. This canvas, for a Dubonnet poster, is a fine example of composition based on simultaneous contrasts in which circular bands of colour are divided up into quadrants. Here rhythm and movement are produced by the eye moving among the repeated colours which are arranged all over the canvas and suggest real movement. Apollinaire described the works of the Orphic artists in this way: "It is the art of painting new compositions with elements not taken from visual reality but created entirely by the artist (...) The works (...) must simultaneously produce sheer aesthetic pleasure, a construction that excites the senses, and a subliminal meaning."

DELAUNAY

Sonia Delaunay

Born in Gradsihsk, the Ukraine, in 1885, she died in Paris in 1979. In Paris she came into contact with the Post-Impressionists and Fauvists. She married Robert Delaunay in 1910 and her most personal works arose as a result of her relationship with the movement known as "Simultaneism", which she developed together with her husband. Coinciding with the outbreak of World War I, the couple travelled to Spain, subsequently exhibiting together at the Sala Mateu Gallery in Madrid (1921). During the 1920s, Sonia Delaunay worked mainly on designing "simultaneist" textiles, which she had began to do in 1912. She took part in the "Exhibition of Decorative Arts" in 1925. After 1930 she turned to painting, and did not return to textile design until 1967, when she worked on new tapestries based on simultaneous colour contrasts.

Jacques Lipchitz
*Escultura,*1915
(Sculpture)
Lead, single piece
123,2 x 27,9 x 29,2 cm
Reg. n° DE-0507

Between 1915 and 1916, Lipchitz, who had began his Cubist works a short time before, managed to create forms which were very close to abstraction. Along these lines is *Escultura* (1915), made with vertical planes complemented and affected by other slanting ones, and thus incorporating the figure in the space around it. This work does, however, retain some references to the human figure in its vertical development and the very slight eye-like mark towards the top. Lipchitz himself described his achievements in works such as this one in this way: (...) "It is a work of pure conception, a non-illusionistic object created from elements invented by the spirit, a sculpture which, retaining its unity, isolates itself in a space created by itself, in a word, an authentic "individual" which, furthermore, carries within itself the basis of a new plastic autonomy."

On the sculptures of this period, Maurice Raynal said: "Delving audaciously into the lyricism of statuary, (Lipchitz) was to merge the idea of human creation with that of nature, revitalising planes and volumes through light and nutritious air, as nature does with trees. (...) From 1915, prudence or rather discipline would lead Jacques Lipchitz to major breakthroughs in his conquest of space and light. And that very prudence would turn out to be fresh fuel for lyricism. (...) These compositions obey both a figure which threatens geometric prudence due to the precariousness of its base, and a mankind whose rules are challenged by the rules of the tree or the bunch of flowers."

LIPCHITZ

Jacques Lipchitz

Born in Druskieniki, Lithuania, in 1891, he died in Capri, Italy, in 1973. He arrived in Paris in 1909, coming into contact with Brancusi and Cubism in 1911, and producing his first works associated with the movement in 1913. He lived in Spain from 1914 to 1915, visiting Mallorca and Madrid with Marie Laurencin and María Blanchard. During this period, he produced works belonging fully to Synthetic Cubism and close to abstract art. On his return to Paris, he came into contact with Juan Gris and, without doubt due to the latter's influence, between 1916 and 1919 produced more figurative works identified with some of Henri Laurens's work. In 1941, during World War II, he took up residence in New York. He moved away from Cubism after 1930.

*T*he second room in the Permanent Collection is devoted to
Juan Gris, who began his career as an artist in the field of
graphic illustration. He came into contact with Picasso when he moved
to Paris in 1906, and he was soon to develop his own form of Cubism
which crystallised around 1913. The pictures from this period quite
clearly reflect the changes that had taken place since his early work.
The volumetric appearance typical of the objects in his first pictures
has almost completely disappeared and space is fragmented through a
grid of horizontal and vertical lines.

Most of the works exhibited in this room belong to the productive
period of between 1915 and 1925. In all of them the initial complexity
of the motifs prompted a more pronounced desire for synthesis with
the objects divested of incidental elements.

In the last years of Gris's life, his works went through major changes,
reflecting a deeper interest in the human form and the possibilities of
its synthetic composition. There is a rich flow of ideas between his oils
and sketches, from which a strong figurative aspect and a classical
form of conception are never absent. Such classicism is possibly Gris's
most personal contribution to Cubism.

7
Juan Gris
Retrato de Josette, 1916
(Portrait of Josette)
Oil on board
116 x 73 cm
Reg. n° 12050

This oil, in which Juan Gris painted his wife, Josette, is a fine example of the artist's knowledge of the painting of previous ages. In relation to this, Christopher Green wrote: "Just like Raynal and Picasso, Gris considered the question of tradition and singled out those masters whose work he felt most drawn to, although he rejected the use of any stylistic mannerism which might indicate a degree or level of indebtedness to the past. He limited himself to inscribing his work within tradition, especially French tradition. This was particularly evident when it came to his choosing the theme of the work, which immediately suggested all kinds of relationships with themes from the past. This occurred especially after 1916, when he made his adaptations of Corot and Cézanne, and was the case of *Retrato de Josette Gris* (painted in the autumn of that year), which can be regarded as a result of *Mujer con mandolina* ('Woman with Mandolin', after Corot). However, it is very likely that he did not make use of any of Corot's figures but simply that of Josette for his portrait, for, as anyone who looks carefully will note, Josette's very posture has an unmistakeable everyday look about it, the same look which Picasso imprinted on his own, pre-war *Mujer con mandolina*. (…)"

8

Juan Gris
Guitarra ante el mar, 1925
(Guitar in Front of the Sea)
Oil on canvas
53 x 64 cm
Reg. n° 05286

J U A N   G R I S

José Victoriano González

Born in Madrid in 1887, he died in Boulogne-sur-Seine, France, in 1927. In 1906, he settled in Paris at the famous Bateau-Lavoir *building, where Picasso and other avant-garde artists were later to take up residence. Around 1910, in an environment dominated by Cubism, Gris produced his first paintings, which were naturalist water-colours deeply influenced by the work of Cézanne. These were followed by other, completely Cubist, works. Between 1913 and 1914, he included collage in his pictures. After the outbreak of World War I, he included dark tones. Gris called the last stage in his development* synthetic *and during this period produced both abstract and figurative compositions.*

On this canvas, which belongs to the painter's last period, Valeriano Bozal made the following observations: "A picture from 1925, by then among the last he was to paint; in its simplicity *Guitarra ante el mar* continues to maintain the 1915 approach. A table on which there is a guitar, a score or a book, a playing card, a piece of fruit and a newspaper with a window behind which is open to a blue sky, the sea with a sailing boat on it and some mountains. The table is the ledge of the window that frames the guitar and is extended in the newspaper, which, by being folded in the air acts as part of the window frame. The score or book stands up, forming another volume of planes in which the card and the piece of fruit stand out, and the guitar, now flat and deep at one and the same time, is segmented.
The system used in this picture by Juan Gris recalls some of the impossible figures analyzed by the psychology of form, but here they are not impossible figures: each of the objects is seen from a different angle, hence their coherence, not their impossibility. The picture gained in compositional simplicity and visual impact, the technical and formal complexity of 1915 having been put aside but not the complexity of its meaning."

*T*he sculptural works of Pablo Picasso apart, Julio González and Pablo Gargallo are the most important Spanish avant-garde figures in this field. Both González and Gargallo were great craftsmen in the field of non-forged metal – avant-garde sculpture's great contribution to art.

This room, dedicated to Pablo Gargallo in the Permanent Collection, exhibits some of his most important works from between the two world wars, when he was at the peak of his career. They demonstrate his mastery in "modelling" space and in making it form as much a part of the work as the material used.

In the late 20s, having put aside the Modernista *connotations of his previous works, Gargallo took up a new form of expression in which first the concave form and later the hollow played an important part as a plastic element or positive volume. All this was possible thanks to Gargallo's work in wrought and cut-out metal.*

An excellent example of this expressiveness are his works on the theme of the prophet, begun in 1904. Having already made sculptures, drawings and sketches for the subject, he finally gave expression to the idea in his largest work, entitled El gran profeta *("The Great Prophet").*

GARGALLO
....
Pablo Gargallo

*Born in Maella, Saragossa,
in 1881, he died in Reus,
Gerona, in 1934. In
Barcelona, he frequented the*
Els Quatre Gats, *where he
became a friend of poets and
painters, including Picasso,
Canals and Nonell. During a
stay in Paris in 1907, he
produced his first cut-out
sheet metal works. Having
returned to Barcelona in
1915, for the next two years
he produced small-format
works only, as he was
suffering from a lung
ailment. From 1927, he
worked in Paris with Julio
González, who taught him
acetylene welding. Thanks to
his particular style, in which
volume and space co-exist in
perfect harmony, Gargallo
was without any doubt one
of the most innovative
sculptors of the century.*

9 ....

Pablo Gargallo
Máscara de Greta Garbo con mechón, 1930
(Mask of Greta Garbo with Lock of Hair)
Wrought iron, single piece
26 x 19 x 12 cm
Reg. n° 00685

Gargallo actually made three different versions – all in sheet
iron – of the famous actress's face. It seems that they were
originally commissioned by a husband and wife who were
art dealers and wished to include the pieces in an exhibition
on Greta Garbo. Gargallo made several preparatory
drawings but the exhibition never took place and the
drawings were mislaid. In spite of this, the artist decided to
continue with the subject and made the three versions from
memory. The piece belonging to the Paris Maxime Blum
Collection depicts the actress wearing a hat and is slightly
smaller than the other two (which belong to the MNCARS
and to a New York private collection). There are only slight
differences between these; the New York version, for
example, has thicker and more curved eyelashes. All,
however, are delicate arabesques of matter floating in space
and it is space itself which gives shape to the sculpture – as
much as, if not more than, the material used.

10
....

Pablo Gargallo
Gran Profeta, 1933
(Great Prophet)
Cast and patinated bronze
245.5 x 75 x 45 cm
Reg. n° 02696

With this piece – he never saw the bronze version as it was cast in 1936 – Pablo Gargallo brought to fruition his largest and most ambitious project. The head of Kiki de Montparnasse, cast in bronze in 1928, had been an excellent exercise in synthesis and the use of space as a sculptural element. But *Gran profeta*, his masterpiece, incorporated the use of modelling and metal casting techniques (both of which had always been traditional in the history of sculpture) into avant-garde plastic art – of which Gargallo was a key figure.

In his work, Gargallo made considerable breakthroughs in the formal research of space and matter, although he never went as far as abstraction. Pierre Courthion said that: "Among the two methods of creation – the concrete and the abstract – he did not resign himself to choosing one or the other, as he was convinced that there was another path – recreation – running below these two and into which they led." In this sculpture, form is recreated through reconstruction with curved planes and spaces cutting through each other – which arises from the decomposition of the Cubist form. Their expressive potential is also determined by the strength and monumentality of the modelling, on which the sculptor stamped the beauty of the material – wrought metal.

*T*he room dedicated to the work of Pablo Picasso consists of several areas corresponding in chronological order to the different stages in the painter's career. The Permanent Collection revolves around this room, due not only to Picasso's importance to the history of 20th-century art but also to the high standard of the works exhibited.

The exhibition begins with Mujer en azul *("Woman in Blue", 1901), situating us at the beginning of the 20th century. Despite the innovative character of this painting, especially in Picasso's conception of colour and the expressiveness of the subject, it is still possible to see traces of the influence of naturalistic Symbolism, a field in which the artist from Malaga was a master.*

In the centre of the room is the work entitled Guernica; *it is a faithful reflection not only of an age but also of painful and dramatic circumstances. This picture was commissioned by the government of the Spanish Republic in 1937 for the Spanish Pavilion at the* Exposition Internationale des Arts et Techniques dans la vie moderne, *commonly known as the 1937 Paris World Fair. Stunned by the news of the bombing of the Basque town (from which the painting takes its title), Picasso painted this huge canvas. Its main subjects are the horse and the bull – from the world of bullfighting – and the mother fleeing with her dead child in her arms. Neither in* Guernica *itself nor in the preparatory studies is there anything that can be identified with the conflict taking place in Spain at the time: there are no weapons, bombs, soldiers or planes. The motifs he chose came from the iconography of his previous works and were always closely connected with events in his private life. This is one reason why* Guernica *has given rise to so many controversial interpretations. In addition to* Guernica *and the studies for it, this room contains works dating from 1912 to 1963, among them* Naturaleza muerta (los pájaros muertos) *["Still Life, (Dead Birds)", 1912], the sculptures* Mujer en el jardín *("Woman in a Garden", 1929-30),* La dama oferente *("Woman with a Vase", 1933) and* El hombre del cordero *("Man with a Lamb", 1943), and the paintings* Figuras al borde del mar *("Figures on a Beach", 1932),* Mujer sentada *("Seated Woman", 1939) and* Mujer sentada en un sillón gris *("Woman Seated in a Grey Chair", 1939), which bring this look at the various periods in Picasso's career to an end.*

PICASSO

Pablo Ruiz Picasso

Born in Malaga in 1881, he died in Mougins, France, in 1973. His works are, without any doubt, the most important of the 20th century and cover a number of interesting periods. Important are the works from his first, so-called Blue Period *(1901-04), and, in his later years, the "Transposition of Museum Masterpieces" series (1955-61), not forgetting: the* Pink Period *(1905-06) – so called because of the colours he used during this time; the* Cubist Period *(1908-16); the period in which his figurative art is strongly reminiscent of the Graeco-Roman style (1917-24); the period in which he associated closely with* Surrealism *(1925-35); or, to mention the years between 1936 and 1945, when his work was influenced by World War II, the time known by some critics as his period of* furious Expressionism. *It was precisely at this time that he produced* Guernica *(1937), his best known and most emblematic work, a heartrending and savage denunciation of the barbarity of war.*

11

Pablo Picasso
Mujer en azul, 1901
(*Woman in Blue*)
Oil on canvas
133 x 100 cm
Reg. n° 01618

Painted during one of the Malaga artist's two short periods in Madrid around the turn of the century, this canvas has a curious story to it. Picasso entered it for the 1901 National Art Exhibition and as it only received an honourable mention, he decided not to collect it at the end of the competition. Time passed and after several decades it was located and rescued from oblivion by Enrique Lafuente Ferrari, to become part of the national collections of contemporary art.

In his memoirs, the great novelist Pío Baroja gave a masterly account of the age and environment in which Picasso painted this type of female portrait: "When he was in Madrid, Pablo Picasso took a studio near Calle Zurbano and devoted his time to painting from memory figures of women with a Parisian air about them, their mouths round and red like wafers...". One of the most beautiful of these figures is without any doubt the anonymous *Mujer de azul* ("Woman in Blue") with her extravagant clothing and enigmatic eyes.

12

Pablo Picasso
Naturaleza muerta (los pájaros muertos), 1912
[Still Life (Dead Birds)]
Oil on canvas
46 x 65 cm
Reg. n° DE-0123

Together with Georges Braque, Picasso was the creator of
Cubism. 1908 saw the beginning of a period in his career which
established a line of research that was to revolutionise the
language of painting and plastic art.

With Cubism reality was analyzed from a fresh viewpoint. Forms
were dislocated, giving rise to a multitude of geometric planes that
extended over the whole surface of the canvas. The inscrutability
of these works is considerable, to such an extent that at times it is
difficult to identify the subject.

After 1912, Picasso painted such works as *Naturaleza muerta (los
pájaros muertos)* in which planes were opened up, printed letters
were included as references to reality, and the subject was alluded
to through its most recognizable and poetic outlines, leading to a
new period called "Synthetic Cubism".

13

Pablo Picasso
La mujer en el jardín, 1929-30
(Woman in a Garden)
Bronze.
209.6 x 116.8 x 81.3 cm
Reg. n° DE-0547

La mujer en el jardín is one of the most outstanding pieces of sculpture to result from the collaboration between Pablo Picasso and Julio González. In the spring of 1928, Picasso visited González at his Paris studio on the Rue de Médéah to see González's forging technique and his work with metals. A year later, in the spring of 1929, they were still collaborating and it was then that *La mujer en el jardín* was begun. Picasso's contribution during the time the two worked together was a large stock of knowledge acquired before 1928, including his knowledge of the ethnological maquettes in the Trocadero Museum, in which pieces of iron and already existing objects were combined. Also important was his knowledge of Pablo Gargallo's wrought iron and copper sculptures reproduced in the magazine *Cahiers d'Art*.
As Werner Spies remarked, all of this shows that pieces such as this one were conceived at a time when Picasso's work echoed, among other sources, the tradition of Spanish sculpting.
In this magnificent sculpture the different pieces are welded together in such a way that the joins are quite visible. One of the most attractive aspects of the work is that the technical media used are clearly noticeable and actually highlighted.

14

Pablo Picasso
La dama oferente, 1933
(Woman with a Vase)
Bronze
220 x 122 x 110 cm
Reg. n° DE-0051

In 1931, Picasso bought a 19th-century mansion in Boisgeloup, on the outskirts of Paris. The building had several large coach houses which he converted into workshops. It was here that he made some of his most interesting three-dimensional works.

La dama oferente – originally of plaster – belongs to this period and was also one of the five Picasso sculptures whose cement cast was exhibited in the Spanish Pavilion at the 1937 Paris World Fair. The model, Marie Thérèse Walter, was his companion during those years, and she also appears in other works of that time. It was originally known as *Femme au vase* ("Woman with a Vase"), but Picasso's last wife, Jacqueline Roque, told a French publication in an interview that its real title was *La porteuse d'offrande*, hence the Spanish name by which it is now known.

Despite having passed virtually unnoticed by experts on Picasso, this piece was to become so important to the painter himself that there is a copy of it on his grave.

Pablo Picasso
Guernica, Paris, 1st May-4th June 1937
Oil on canvas
349.3 x 776.6 cm
Reg. n° 0050

Since it was painted, this great canvas has given rise to many different
observations. The one below dates from 1938, when *Guernica*, on one of its
European tours to raise money for Spanish refugees, arrived in London after
the Paris World Fair. On this occasion, it inspired Herbert Read to say:
[Guernica] "is a monument to destruction, a cry of indignation and horror
intensified by the spirit of the genius. Not only *Guernica*, but Spain, not only
Spain, but Europe are symbolised in this allegory. It is our modern Calvary,
the agony – amidst bombed-out ruins – of human tenderness and faith. It is a
religious picture, painted perhaps not with the same kind but with the same
degree of fervour that inspired Grünewald and the Master of the Avignon
Pietà, Van Eyck and Bellini. It is not enough to compare the Picasso of this
picture with the Goya of the *Disasters*. Goya was also a great artist, and a
great humanist; but his reactions were individualistic, his tools were irony,
satire, ridicule. Picasso is more universal: his symbols are trivial, like
Homer's, Dante's, Cervantes's symbols."

Pablo Picasso
Mujer sentada en un sillón gris, 1939
(Woman Seated in a Grey Armchair)
Oil on canvas
130 x 97 cm
Reg. n° D-0305

Dated 1st April 1939, this canvas belongs to the period in
Picasso's work connected with the Spanish Civil War, an event
which was to influence the painter's production until some time
after the end of World War II. In the 1930s, his female portraits
were frequent, and Picasso painted Marie Thérèse Walter and
Dora Maar many times. In this picture, painted in his artistic prime,
Picasso depicted a subject he had already dealt with in the 20s
and which he was to go on using during the 40s and 50s – a
woman sitting in an armchair. Here the artist synthesized the
plastic idiom he had previously used. He built up the figure with
blocks of colour, crowning it with a violently distorted face – as if it
is crying out – which, together with the position of the arms,
recalls the preparatory studies of 1937 for *Guernica.*

Pablo Picasso
El hombre del cordero, 1943
(Man with a Lamb)
Plaster, single piece
222,5 x 78 x 78 cm
Reg. n° D-0307

Werner Spies made the following observation on this work: "*El hombre del cordero* is one of Picasso's most surprising sculptures. It is not only a very large piece, fully modelled and reminiscent of Rodin, but also a figure governed by traditional laws. Although the old model is present, Picasso does not follow it literally, instead submitting it to a characteristic modification. The rigidness, noticeable even in the position of the legs, gives the figure a certain consistency. It is a form of rigidness also seen in Rodin's nude for Joan of Arc. Here and there movement seems petrified. The left hand presses the feet of the lamb, depriving it of freedom of movement and forcing it to sit up in a convulsed gesture. The motif of the sacrifice of the lamb was crystallised little by little, as is evident from the studies of between March and August 1943."

*T*his room is dedicated to the works of Joan Miró, particularly his pictures. The exhibition begins with a number of oils painted when he was in closest contact with the Surrealist group, between 1923 and 1929, although it is true that Miró always remained independent of groups and ideologies. At this time he painted a number of Automatic pictures and in 1929-30 began on his collages. This process led him to take an interest in the object in itself and resulted in his famous surrealistic sculptures. 1934 saw the appearance of his tormented monsters, which gave way in 1938 to the consolidation of his plastic vocabulary.

His final period was approximately from 1967 until his death in 1983. It is characterised by large dimensions, gestural aspects, the freshness with which his pictures were painted, the special attention he paid to the material he used, and by the influence of informalism. The iconographic repertoire of Miró's later years was not greatly different from that of his earlier periods. The motifs were the same (women, birds, stars, constellations, the sun, the moon...), but the importance he attached at this time to the subject in itself was relative, for what really interested Miró was the point of connection between the world of the conceptual and the world of artistic expression and, above all, the way in which this could be captured on the canvas.

MIRÓ

Joan Miró

Born in Barcelona, in 1893, he died in Palma de Mallorca in 1983. In 1919, he made his first trip to Paris, after which he spent various winters there, spending the summers in Montroig. In the French capital he came into contact with the avant-garde and became a firm friend of Picasso's. He settled in Mallorca in 1941. After starting out as a painter and plastic artist with what is known as his "detallista" period, Miró became influenced by Cubism. He then developed a pictorial language all his own with motifs reduced to enigmatic symbols and a personal style close to Surrealism.

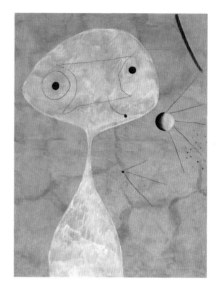

18

Joan Miró
***Hombre con pipa*, 1925**
(*Man with a Pipe*)
Oil on canvas
146 x 114 cm
Reg. n° 11003

In this oil painting, as in subsequent ones, such as *Sin título I* ("Untitled I") and *Sin título III* ("Untitled III", both dated 1973), Miró paid tribute to the colour blue, which majestically occupies almost all of the canvas. Alexandre Cirici compared this colour with another normally used by Miró as a background for his compositions – brown: ..."Once the 'Miró language' was developed, two colours became dominant as backgrounds: blue and brown. It should be noted that the blue was often extremely pure, while the brown tended to contain a whole range of tones and patiently applied textures. In many cases, the blue had no qualms about demonstrating the work process, the brush-stroke. The brown tended to be impasted more conscientiously. The blue is like a writing of the concept *blue* which does not shy away from calligraphy. The brown is like an immediate material presence. Blue and brown are two different places: the former is thought out, devised, it is the blue of intangible things; the latter is made, and impasted, it is the brown of tangible things."

19

Joan Miró
Retrato II, 1938
(Portrait II)
Oil on canvas
162 x 130 cm
Reg. nº 08591

Painted during the period subsequent to Miró's closest
association with Surrealism (1924-26) and when he began
to see his personal plastic idiom take shape, this imposing,
monumental canvas has been described by Jacques Dupin,
the expert par excellence on Miró's work, in the following
way: "If *Retrato I* still appears to be dripping, dizzy and
laden down with the dross of an appalling period, then
Retrato II is expression purified and simplified to the point of
severity. Balanced on a Prussian-blue background, linked by
a thread, are the semi-circular mass of the body and the
flattened circle of the head. The subdued, subtly arranged
colours (red, orange, violet and green) occupy strictly
defined surfaces. The wispy form on the face vaguely recalls
a nose and eyes and corresponds to the same kind of line
made on the body by the division of colours. The absence
of detail is astonishing. Miró only asks the colour (in pure
but subdued tones) to enliven this austere, somewhat
indifferent, strangely absent figure."

*C*onsidered by David Smith – the most important American sculptor of the Abstract Expressionist generation – as the "Father of all sculpture in iron of this century", Julio González created works whose importance is based on two basic factors: the use of iron as an art material and the parity of the void and solid as plastic elements in his three-dimensional work.

He began sculpting at the turn of the century, producing masks, heads and nudes in repoussé copper in a style close to Modernisme and Noucentisme. His collaboration with Pablo Picasso, which began in 1928, gave a new impetus to his sculptures. During this period, he began to use the medium that would bring a revolutionary change to his works – wrought cutout, curved and welded iron. The importance he attached to empty space as an integral part of the sculpture can also be appreciated during this period.

Some of the most important works exhibited in this room come from the artist's later or mature period as opposed to other works from the same period in which delicacy of form is stressed. The most outstanding feature of these is a certain tendency towards stasis.

One part of this room is dedicated to the American sculptor David Smith – mentioned at the beginning of this page – whose works were directly inspired by Julio González's ideas.

20

Julio González
Cabeza llamada
"El conejo", c. 1930
(*Head Called*
"The Rabbit")
Wrought and welded
iron, single piece
33 x 17.5 x 11.5 cm
Reg. n° 10351

As Jörn Merkert, author of the *catalogue raisonné* of Julio
González's sculptures, states, this work belongs to the
series of pieces made with cutout metal sheet around 1930.
All of these were mounted on irregularly-shaped bases of
calcareous stone, a material which he was also to use on
his *ronde-bosse* heads.

Once again, to suggest tri-dimensionality, the sculptor used
not only the opposites of light and shadow but also, and
above all, the contrast between matter and space. The
empty and the full are thus on an equal par as far as
sculptural materials are concerned.

The idea that this bust, which is not lacking in irony and
humour, might be a self-portrait, cannot be dismissed,
especially if we take into account the thick eyebrows and
the very characteristic moustache – both of which were
distinguishing features of Julio González's.

GONZÁLEZ

Julio González

Born in Barcelona in 1876, he died in Arcueil, Paris, in 1942. Thanks to his work as an apprentice welder in the French capital, he learned acetylene welding, which was to prove decisive for all his subsequent work as a sculptor. From 1928, his work, hitherto clearly reminiscent of Cubism, began to develop towards the abstract forms which he called "drawings in space". In the late 20s and early 30s, he worked with Pablo Picasso and in 1937 made his famous Montserrat *sculpture for the Spanish Pavilion at the 1937 Paris World Fair.*

21

Julio González
***Mujer sentada I*, c. 1935**
(Seated Woman I)
Wrought and welded iron, single piece
118.5 x 38 x 59 cm
Reg. nº 10757

For *Mujer sentada I* – a key work among those which belong to the MNCARS – Julio González drew a number of sketches in 1935 and 1936 (some of which also belong to the Museum Collection). This is the first sculpted version of a subject on which González based another piece, which belongs to the *Musée Nationale d'Art Moderne de la Ville de Paris*, and is dated around 1935-36.

Mujer sentada I is a completely abstract work, although González never ceased to observe reality. It reveals a new interest in cubic and volumetric forms which, according to Margit Rowell, was suggested to Julio González by the work of Alberto Magnelli, whom the Spanish artist had met in Paris around 1934. The result, previously absent in González's metal works, was the two versions of *Mujer sentada*, in which Magnelli's full, stone forms – although González used hollow volumes of welded metal – were adapted to the human figure.

*T*his room exhibits a number of works by four artists – Jean Arp, Alexander Calder, Vassily Kandinsky and André Masson – exponents of the various paths in painting and the plastic arts that existed between Surrealism and abstraction from 1920 on. André Masson, a painter linked to the French Surrealist movement, often fell back on one of this group's commonest themes – metamorphosis. Here the changes that turn one motif into another are reflected by means of associations of ideas without logic, giving rise to stimulating, disturbing images.

In his first works, Jean Arp turned to Dada aesthetics, but he gradually moved away from this movement to associate with Surrealist circles. His works evoked the continuous flux of nature and its constant process of transformation. Always on the borderline between Surrealism and abstraction, Alexander Calder began by including motors in his sculptures, but subsequently replaced them with simple systems using the displacement of air as a means of generating movement.

Finally, there are works by Vassily Kandinsky, an artist of fundamental importance to the abstract movement who in his later years turned to an original, very lyrical, form of abstraction. Kandinsky's use of colour and his linear forms were the basic ingredients of a new way of painting whose theoretical bases he was to expound in various publications.

CALDER

Alexander Calder

Born in Lawton, Pennsylvania, U.S.A., in 1898, he died in New York in 1976. His first sculptures, produced in Paris in 1926, were very favourably received by various personalities from the world of culture, and from then on both the United States and the French capital became his habitual places of residence. In 1931, he joined the Abstraction-Création *group. It was also at this time that he made his first motor-driven metal constructions, which Marcel Duchamp dubbed* Mobiles. *In 1933, he devised a new type of* Mobile *whose movement was generated by the displacement of air. In addition to his sculptures, Calder painted, designed jewellery and tapestries and was an engraver.*

Alexander Calder
Constelación, c. 1940-1943
(Constellation)
Painted wood and steel wire
90 x 67.5 x 80 cm
Reg. n° 11051

The light forms which make up this piece from the *Constelaciones* ("Constellations") series and their slow swaying motion on contact with the air, reveal the personal poetic spirit of Calder's work. The artist himself said in reference to his works: "From the beginning of my abstract work – and even though this may not seem to be the case – I felt that there was no better model to choose than that of the Universe... Spheres of different sizes, densities, colours and volumes, floating in space, clouds moving by, sprinkled with water, air currents, viscosities and smells – all of the greatest variety and disparity."

ARP

Jean Arp

Born in Strasbourg, France, in 1886, he died in Basle, Switzerland, in 1966. Together with Tristan Tzara, Hugo Ball, Marcel Janco and Huelsenbeck, he founded the Dada movement in 1916 at the Cabaret Voltaire in Zurich. His first abstract works date from around 1915, although his work developed approximately one year later into a series of Dada painted wood reliefs which were extremely simple in structure. In 1930, he began to produce ronde-bosse sculptures by now closer to Surrealist postulates. During his last period of development the void played an extremely important part in the overall conception of his work.

23

Jean Arp
Objetos colocados según las leyes del azar, 1926
(Objects Placed According to the Laws of Chance)
Painted wood
37 x 57 x 6.4 cm.
Reg nº 11064

Arp made his first wood relief in 1915 in a creative process whose origin lay in the techniques of collage and assemblage. In "So the Circle was Closed", in which Arp considered his own work, he spoke of the origin of pieces such as the relief *Objetos colocados según las leyes del azar*, painted one year after the Surrealist group's first exhibition at the Pierre Gallery in Paris (in which he also exhibited). He wrote, "I went on developing the collage technique, turning my mind away from composition and giving myself up to automatic execution. I called it 'working according to the law of chance', the law that contains all others and which we cannot understand, just as we don't understand the primaeval cause that makes any type of life bud and can only be experienced through total surrender to the unconscious mind. I maintained that whoever obeyed that law would create life in a pure state."
Such ideas impregnate all of Jean Arp's poetic and artistic creation. Arp said, "I don't pretend to copy nature. I don't want to reproduce it. I want to create it just as a plant produces fruit..."

S alvador Dalí painted his first pictures in 1917 and 1918,
influenced during this initial period by several tendencies.
The period between 1922 and 1923 and approximately up to 1928
saw his so-called Cubist phase, in which the influence of Cubism was
mixed with the evocation of motifs from metaphysical painting.
During this phase, one year – 1925 – is particularly interesting, for,
due to his close relationship with Federico García Lorca, he entered
what has been called his "Lorquiano" period. Also in 1925, Dalí
painted beautiful canvases in a classical style subsequently taken up
by movements such as the Neue Sachlichkeit *and* Valori Plastici.
In 1927, he again became deeply interested in Cubism, but with a
style all his own and adapted to the laws of his own personality.
Subsequently, in 1928, he settled in Paris, where great changes took
place in his form of art. In the French capital he came into contact
with the Surrealists. At the beginning he painted a number of almost
completely abstract oils. In 1929, he painted what were to be his best-
known Surrealist works, in which abstract motifs gave way to
elaborate figurativeness. The most innovative aspect, however, came
with his invention of a new system allowing him access to the images
of his subconscious – the paranoiac critical *method.*
The works chosen for the room dedicated to Salvador Dalí illustrate
the main creative periods in the painter's career.

DALÍ

Salvador Dalí

Born in 1904, in Figueras,
Gerona, where he died in
1989. Having struck up a
friendship with Luis Buñuel
and Federico García Lorca in
Madrid, he moved to Paris
in 1928, where he came into
contact with the Surrealist
group and became one of its
leading figures. At this time
he also worked with Buñuel
on two very famous films:
Un Chien Andalou *and*
L'Age d'or. *In 1934, he*
broke away from the
Surrealist movement, not
without leaving it an
extremely important
legacy – the method he
himself described as
paranoiac critical. *In*
addition to his paintings,
he is famous for his
drawings, his jewellery,
furniture, and fashion
designs, and his sets for
cinema, stage and ballet.

24

Salvador Dalí
Muchacha en la ventana, 1925
(Girl at the Window)
Oil on cardboard
105 x 74.5 cm
Reg. n° 02157

In a 1949 publication, Ana María Dalí, the painter's sister,
recalled her long sessions as Dalí's model: ..."The portraits
my brother painted of me during that time are countless.
Many of them were mere studies of curls and an always
bare shoulder. He painted patiently and indefatigably and I
never tired of posing for him, as sitting still and in silence
has never bored me. (...) During all the hours I was his
model, I never grew tired of looking at that landscape which
became part of me forever. Because he always painted me
close to a window, and my eyes had time to take in every
single detail."

Salvador Dalí
El gran masturbador, 1929
(The Great Masturbator)
Oil on canvas
110 x 150.5 cm
Reg. n° 11140

The symbol par excellence of Dalí's sexual obsessions, this picture was mentioned by the painter himself in his most famous publication *The Secret Life of Salvador Dalí* (1975): ..."It was a great head as if of wax, very rosy cheeks, long eyelashes, and a great nose pressed against the ground. This face had no mouth and instead I had stuck a huge locust there. The locust's abdomen was decomposing and was full of ants. Several of these were running through the space that should have been filled by the non-existent mouth of that great distressed face whose head ended in 1900s-style architecture and ornamentation. The title of the painting was *The Great Masturbator*."

*I*n Paris in 1924, the poet André Breton issued what was to be the first Surrealist Manifesto. *More than anything else, the new movement inherited from its predecessor, Dada, the deep conviction that reason was no more than an irritating obstacle which hindered the development of creativity.*

Taking Sigmund Freud's key work The Interpretation of Dreams, *published in 1900, as his starting point, Breton came to the conclusion that the only way to sever ties with reason was to gain access to the subconscious.*

Having perfected the theory, all that was left was to put it into practice. The group of Surrealist poets discovered how to "penetrate" the subconscious in two ways and these became the Surrealistic techniques par excellence: Automatism, *which, broadly speaking, consisted of drawing or writing without any logic, allowing the hand or the paintbrush to move freely and without control; and* dépaysement réfléchi *("reflexive disorientation"), a process in which the images that emerged from the subconscious were captured and unconnected objects were placed in perfectly logical spaces.*

In the room of the Permanent Collection dedicated to this movement, works by the Spanish artist Oscar Domínguez have been included together with others by foreign artists – Joseph Cornell, Max Ernst, René Magritte and Yves Tanguy. A piece produced jointly by Salvador Dalí and Man Ray is also exhibited.

MAN RAY

Man Ray

*Born in Philadelphia,
U.S.A., in 1890, he died in
Paris in 1978. He attended
the National Academy of
Design, New York. Around
1916, he associated with the
Dada group, subsequently
taking part in their
exhibitions. He collaborated
with Marcel Duchamp on
the publication of* The Blind
Man *and* Rongwrong
*magazines. In the 1920s, he
moved to Paris and joined
the Surrealist group. During
this decade he also devised a
new art process – the*
rayograph *– in which
photographic images were
made without a camera by
placing an object on
emulsified paper exposed to
light. His paintings,
photographs,* rayographs
*and "unpleasant objects"
were the main aspects of his
work, which is generally
classified as belonging to
Surrealism.*

26

Salvador Dalí
Man Ray
***Retrato de Joella*, 1933-1934**
(Portrait of Joella)
Oil, water-based paint and plaster
40.5 x 17.5 x 18 cm
Reg. n° 11943

Valeriano Bozal remarked on various aspects of this work:
"The head that Man Ray had made was completely
transformed. Dalí painted various motifs that changed its
sense. On the right cheek, a landscape of clouds with an
immense open space and a small figure casting an
excessively large shadow; in sharp contrast, on the left side
of the face, painted as if it were a brick wall, he placed an
opening through which the continuation of the landscape on
the right could be seen.(...)
"The consistency of the plaster, its smoothness as a
material and a surface, was transformed with Dalí's painting;
the generic and the flatness of the classicist mould gave
way to an allegorical figure."

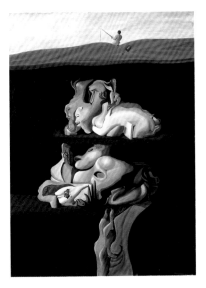

27

Oscar Domínguez
Cueva de guanches, 1935
(Guanche Cave)
Oil on canvas
81 x 60 cm
Reg. nº 10528

DOMÍNGUEZ

Oscar Domínguez

Born in La Laguna, Tenerife, in 1906, he died in Paris in 1957. In 1927, he travelled to the French capital, where he began his training as a painter. His first works were connected with Surrealism and date from 1929, when he settled permanently in Paris. His Surrealist works, along the lines of those of René Magritte and Salvador Dalí, led to his so-called cosmic period of between 1938 and 1939, which is characterised by the discovery of a personal language by then somewhat removed from Surrealism. His last works clearly display the influence of Picasso's Cubism.

"The impact made by this picture is due to the composition appearing from an angle like that of a deep black stratigraphic cut in whose centre a number of limp bodies and faces are illuminated; these are the redoubt of the desires and the passions and they can be opened, for the key at the top symbolises the exit from that inhibited world into the light. The character quietly fishing on the surface may well be the artist. The violent contrast between the world of reason and the world of the instincts is achieved by setting out the composition within two horizontal bands. The lower band is painted in deep black and occupies three quarters of the picture (and symbolises the world of the instincts), whereas the upper band is strongly lit and represents the rational world."

This is how Fernando of Castro described *Cueva de guanches*, an oil painting from the group of compositions in which the Canarian painter nostalgically recalled his homeland. This group also includes *Recuerdo de una isla* ("Memory of an Island") and *Mariposas perdidas en las montañas* ("Butterflies Lost in the Mountains").

*I*n this room, works by one of the most important Spanish film-makers of this century – Aragon's Luis Buñuel – are exhibited. By including his work in the Permanent Collection, the Museo Nacional Centro de Arte Reina Sofía *wishes not only to pay tribute to Buñuel, but also to acknowledge the importance of film-making by placing it on a par with painting and the plastic arts. The relationship between this director's work and the different artistic manifestations of his time is well known. In this sense, the films shown in this room,* Un chien andalou *(1929) and* L'Age d'or *(1930), belong wholly to Surrealism.*

Buñuel came to Madrid as a young man, and lived at the Residencia de Estudiantes. *He subsequently moved to Paris, where he studied film direction under Jean Epstein. In 1929, he came into contact with the Surrealist group, keeping up a close relationship with them until 1932.*

In 1946, he settled in Mexico, where he made several films. In 1960, after 24 years of exile, he returned to Spain to make one of his best-known films – Viridiana *(1961). In 1969, he made* Tristana *in* Toledo. *He died in Mexico City at the age of 83.*

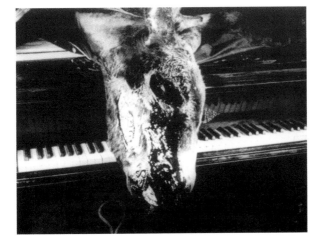

Luis Buñuel
Un perro andaluz, 1929
(An Andalusian Dog)
Titles: Salvador Dalí and Luis Buñuel
Directed by: Luis Buñuel
Sets: Pierre Schildknecht
Photography: Albert Duverger
Footage: 432 m.
Running time: 24 min., black and
white; silent

In his autobiography, dated 1939, Luis Buñuel made the
following remarks on *Un chien andalou*: "In the film, the
aesthetics of Surrealism are combined with some of Freud's
discoveries. The film was totally in keeping with the basic
principle of the school, which defined Surrealism as 'Psychic
Automatism, unconscious, capable of returning to the mind
its true functions, beyond any form of control by reason,
morality or aesthetics'."

B U Ñ U E L

Luis Buñuel

*Born in Calanda, Teruel, in
1900, he died in Mexico City
in 1983. In 1917, he moved
to Madrid, living at the*
Residencia de
Estudiantes, *where he
struck up a friendship with
Dalí and García Lorca. In
1925, he settled in Paris and
studied cinema direction
under Jean Epstein. There
he also associated with the
Surrealist movement. He
made his first film,* Un
Chien Andalou, *in 1929,
and his last,* That Obscure
Object of Desire, *in 1977.
Buñuel created his own
personal imagery – linked to
themes related to the look,
desire, and death – in films
of irrefutably high quality.*

Luis Buñuel
La edad de oro, 1930
(The Golden Age)
Script: Luis Buñuel and Salvador Dalí
Directed by: Luis Buñuel
Sets: Pierre Schildknecht and Serge Pimenoff
Photography: Albert Duverger
Footage: 1715 m.
Running time: 63 min., black and white

Agustín Sánchez Vidal said the following about *L'Age d'or*:
"When all is said and done, in spite of the similarities with *Un chien andalou*, *L'Age d'or* is a more kinetic film, more cinematic – in short, more Buñuel. To demonstrate this, we shall limit ourselves to a single example, pursuing it throughout the film – and along the same lines as those with which Sigmund Freud analyzed the scope of failed actions in *The Psychopathology of Everyday Life* – a gesture that displays the set of deep psychic functions of the situations and characters. Thanks to those apparently insignificant gestures, a bridge was built between intangible subliminal fluxes and their materialization in gestures and objects. It comes as no surprise that Buñuel and Dalí turned to these in order to display that connection between physical and psychic Automatism. Except that the painter tended to capture them statically, whereas the film-maker surprised them in motion."

*A*fter World War I, the position of European art was extremely complex. In some countries the avant-garde movements adopted a deeply radical character and committed themselves to criticising and changing society.

Accompanying these movements we also find a "return to order", which in some countries became considerably nationalistic in nature. The "return to order" movement considered it necessary to bring an end to the chaos or disorder caused by Cubism and its derivatives. However, this position could not be a homogeneous one, for the noteworthy differences between the French, Italian and German manifestations were aesthetic as well as ideological.

In Spain, where artistic renovation was meagre, the situation was equally complex and always involved the temptation to define modernity as eclecticism – as was evident at the Exposición de los Artistas Ibéricos held in the Retiro Park, Madrid, in May 1925. In this Permanent Collection room a variety of very different works are exhibited, reflecting the situation described above. They include exhibits by: Aurelio Arteta, Roberto Fernández Balbuena, María Blanchard, Francisco Bores, Pancho Cossío, Pablo Gargallo, Daniel González, Mateo Hernández, Manolo Hugué, Nicolás de Lekuona, Maruja Mallo, José Moreno Villa, Benjamín Palencia, Alfonso Ponce de León, Olga Sacharoff, Alberto Sánchez, Ángeles Santos, Joaquín Sunyer, José de Togores, José María Ucelay, Adriano del Valle, Daniel Vázquez Díaz and Rosario de Velasco.

MALLO

Maruja Mallo

Born in Tuy, Pontevedra, in 1902, she died in Madrid in 1995. She was an active member of the avant-garde circles of pre-war Madrid, attending the gatherings of the period and becoming a friend of most of the best-known artists, poets and painters. During the pre-war period, her style went through two very different phases, bright colours being typical of the first, and the use of dark, subdued tones more characteristic of her work during the 1930s. Generally speaking, her work can be classified as belonging to the Spanish figurative art of the 20s and 30s with constant allusions to Surrealism.

30

Maruja Mallo
La verbena, 1927
(The Festival)
Oil on canvas
119 x 166 cm
Reg. n° 01985

At her solo exhibition organised by Ortega y Gasset in the rooms of the *Revista de occidente* in 1928, Maruja Mallo included the four oils of her series dedicated to the Madrid festivals. Consuelo de la Gándara described this painting, which belongs to the MNCARS, in great detail: ..."Now the third one. In this, there is an outburst of mordant sarcasm. The composition is even more motley than the previous ones; the *verbena* elements have given up the limelight; the characters have multiplied; that "Dark Spain" makes its appearance and only a few tender notes, one being the sleigh gliding through a landscape of snow and firs in the distance, recall the *Fiesta*. Two pairs of figures dominate the picture: the "giants" depicting the king and his lawyer (bearers of cardboard chimneys by way of sceptres) and the woman and policeman with their Valencian *Ninot* faces. Around these, other, secondary, figures act as a contrast: the girls with throbbing bosoms, full of youthful life, starting to run, and the sailors with dreamy looks on their faces. (...)"

31 ....
Alfonso Ponce de León
Accidente, 1936
(Accident)
Oil on canvas
158 x 188 cm
Reg. n° 00745

PONCE DE LEÓN
....
Alfonso Ponce de León

*Born in Malaga in 1900, he
died in Madrid in 1936.
Having completed his art
studies, he began to associate
with the Madrid avant-
garde circles. In the late
1920s, he travelled to Paris.
His support for culture
extended to fields other than
painting: in 1932, he was an
active member of the
editorial staff of* Arte
magazine, *published by the*
Sociedad de Artistas
Ibéricos; *he designed
costumes and sets for the* La
Barraca *university theatre
group; and he made one
incursion into the film world
with* Niños *("Children",
1931). His paintings can be
categorised as belonging to
Surrealism and Magic
Realism.*

This *Accident* (1936), by Ponce de León, is in fact a
premonitory self-portrait in which the author seems to sense
his own imminent and tragic death, which occurred that
same year.
Although the scene cannot be considered as strictly
surrealistic but closer to Magic Realism, it contains certain
dreamlike connotations. This sensation is heightened
through several details, such as the very strange position of
the body with the legs lost between the car's headlights and
bodywork, the light – which does not come from the
headlight – illuminating the victim, and, above all, the
unusual way in which the subject – probably already dead –
points to his forehead with a blood-stained index finger.
The powerful beam of light which defines outlines and casts
mysterious shadows is also one of the most disconcerting
elements in the picture, giving it an almost ghostly
appearance. The lush vegetation bursting in on the
right-hand side and reminiscent of *Le Douanier* Rousseau's
"plant tapestries", is yet another factor which unsettles the
observer.

*T*he room of the Permanent Collection dedicated to the
Asturian painter Luis Fernández contains all of the artist's
works in the Museum Collection. Fernández moved to Paris in 1924,
learning the language of some of the main avant-garde movements –
abstraction, Cubism and Surrealism.

In the 1930s, his work took the form of geometric abstract art
characterised by strict formal treatment of the elements. He often
worked with lines and planes of subdued colours which stood out
against a geometrically arranged surface.

Later, during the years of the Spanish Civil War and World War II,
his work developed into a form of expression related to Surrealism. It
was during this time that he painted compositions with violently
distorted animal heads.

In the 50s, Fernández began to paint series of works with the same
subjects – skulls, roses and doves. In these fully mature pictures,
Fernández's painting revolves around three, seemingly contradictory
components: the tradition of the Spanish painting of the Golden Age,
the landscape painting of German Romanticism and the formal
renewal taking place in the art which was developing in Paris.

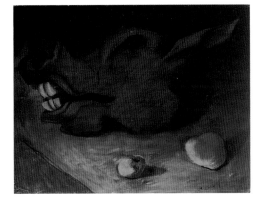

FERNÁNDEZ
Luis Fernández

Born in Oviedo in 1900, he died in Paris in 1973. In 1909, he moved to Barcelona, where he attended the Escuela de Bellas Artes. In 1924, he travelled to Paris, where he came into contact with the local avant-garde art movements and associated with artists such as Braque, Le Corbusier, Lipchitz and Picasso. He wrote articles for the magazines AC and Cahiers d'Art. Fernández's first works were abstract but later developed towards Surrealism. During the 40s he returned to figurative art, focusing his iconography on still lifes, landscapes and animals. His works of art were complemented by a noteworthy theoretical output.

Luis Fernández
Cabeza de res con manzanas, 1939
(Animal Head with Apples)
Oil on paper glued to board
50 x 65 cm
Reg. n° DE-0503

Luis Fernández's theoretical work was noteworthy and is complementary to his works of art. He sometimes analyzed the different aspects – both technical and formal – of his pictorial work.

The statement below confirms this; it comes from the magazine *Cahiers d'Art* and was made by Fernández in 1936: "My preoccupation with the flawless execution and the durability of the picture, is, among other things, a desire for a smooth surface on which no brush-stroke is visible; which means, apart from all else, the partial implementation of an often expressed wish for the picture to reach out to the observer through the emotion emanating from it and for the craftsmanship that has gone into it to be invisible. Thus, in any work, once it is finished, all traces of the tools should have disappeared and the object produced should appear to be a kind of miracle."

33

Luis Fernández
La rosa, c. **1962-1965**
(The Rose)
Gouache on paper
22 x 30 cm
Reg. n° DE-0506

In the passage below, René Ménard remarked on the personal spirit which instilled the work of Luis Fernández when he returned definitively to figurative art:
"Fernández has made a revelation to me.
He takes his inspiration from reality, but begins by killing it. To return it to life, he slowly, through a kind of hallucinatory ascesis, abstracts secondary forms from it in which the object is recognized, recreated from the only light condensed specifically on each and every one of its surfaces and for each and every one of the relationships which unite it to the space in which its presence is exercised (...) That is why a picture by this painter etches itself so extraordinarily on the memory, as if the spirit were as naturally the support as the painted surface which somewhere materializes it."

*T*he names of Alberto Sánchez and Benjamín Palencia are
linked to the School of Vallecas. *However, the "School"
was no more than an aesthetic approach attempting to retrieve the
texture of nature, earth and stones, the ruts of the countryside... The
two artists outlined this approach during their walks in the fields
around Vallecas, an area which at that time lay outside Madrid.
Alberto began working as a sculptor in 1925, developing his most
personal form of aesthetics within the* School of Vallecas. *At this
time he produced a large number of works inspired by the Castilian
countryside and its traditions and imbued with the plastic language of
the European avant-garde. Exhibited here alongside works of this type
are others from the sculptor's Russian period in the 50s and 60s, and
yet others in which he returned to the aesthetic approach of his
Spanish period using new materials.*

*Benjamín Palencia was born and bred in the country and, like
Alberto, was self-taught. The importance of the materials he used in
his paintings during his period with the* School of Vallecas *is
evident. Both unusual and modern, they included sand, clay and ash.
Present in Palencia's work is the influence of key figures from
contemporary art, such as Klee and Kandinsky, and that of the
painters of the* Paris School.

SÁNCHEZ

Alberto Sánchez

Born in Toledo in 1895, he died in Moscow in 1962. A self-taught artist, in 1926 he created the School of Vallecas *with a number of other painters. From 1938 until his death he lived in Moscow. Having produced a number of works directly inspired by observing* nature, around 1926 he entered his mature period, which continued until 1937. From 1955, after a long period dedicated exclusively to teaching and set design, he returned to sculpting, using a number of new materials including sheet iron and wood pulp in his work, although he was never to renounce his characteristic style of the 20s and 30s.

Alberto Sánchez
El pueblo español tiene un camino que conduce a una estrella, 1937
(The Spanish People Have a Road that Leads to a Star)
Painted black plaster
184.5 x 32 x 33 cm
Reg. n° 11424

Alberto, who as an acknowledged member of the avant-garde and supporter of the Republican government had been commissioned a large sculpture for the Spanish Pavilion at the 1937 Paris World Fair, had already made a complete maquette which in itself was an original piece and is now exhibited in the Permanent Collection.

The final version, exhibited in the entrance to the Pavilion, disappeared during his return to Spain after the Fair.

The subject of a wide variety of interpretations, it has even been said that this stylised monolith was conceived in accordance with an obviously political symbology, as it imitated a clenched fist. However, it seems much more likely that, like the rest of Alberto's works, this piece had distinct Surrealistic roots and was a typical metamorphosis in which animal and plant life merged.

PALENCIA

Benjamín Palencia

Born in Barrax, Albacete, in 1894, he died in Madrid in 1980. In 1909, he moved to Madrid, founding the School of Vallecas *in 1926. After an initial period in which his figurative work was very close to that of Salvador Dalí's 1925 pieces, he turned towards a form of more schematic composition deeply influenced by Cubism. 1929-1930 saw a new pictorial period with strong surrealistic connotations, followed, after the Spanish Civil War, by another known as* Favismo Ibérico.

35

Benjamín Palencia
Toros (Tauromaquia), 1933
[Bulls (Bullfighting)]
Oil on canvas
79.5 x 95 cm
Reg. nº 06123

Self-taught, a friend and companion of the most prominent members of the Spanish avant-garde in the 20s and 30s, Benjamín Palencia founded the *School of Vallecas*, his aim being to revitalise the arts scene in Spain with a reassessment of the concept of landscape as his starting point. José Corredor Matheos summed up Palencia's artistic thinking in a reference to this canvas, a fine example of his aesthetics during the *School of Vallecas* period: [In] "*Tauromaquia* (1933) forms seem to have been cut down to the bone. Stripped bare, they stand erect as symbols. They sing of the archetypal and the essential aspects of a landscape, the Castilian landscape, that of La Mancha in particular. They are scarecrows or human and animal forms reduced to their frames, to their lines of force, close to popular tradition. They form part of the landscape from which they came and, at the same time, Prometheus-like they oppose it. Looking at them as pure plastic art may be enough for us. Perhaps this is their main value. In these times of passionate avant-garde adventure, this is the most important thing, although what also counts, of course, is what in a certain sense they *mean* – in this case the evocation of a landscape, to which homage is paid."

The first part of the Permanent Collection ends with a room dedicated to sculpture. With bronzes by Joan Miró as the main focus, there are also pieces by Angel Ferrant, Leandre Cristòfol and Ramón Marinel.lo.

Of Miró's sculptures the bronzes are the most important and also the most numerous. They date from the second half of the 60s, when Miró returned, to a certain extent, to the spirit of the objects of his surrealist period. For these sculptures Miró began by collecting worthless objects of all kinds, choosing at random those which most attracted his attention. He made changes to these and placed them together. Before transferring them to the final material to be used – bronze using the cire perdue *method – Miró once again intervened, making lines or marks on the wax mould. Finally, the actual smelting and patination of the bronze was a craft process which Joan Miró carried out with great care.*

Next to Miró's sculptures are works by Angel Ferrant, who in his Barcelona period made pieces related to Surrealism. There are also pieces by two other artists linked to Spanish Surrealism – Leandre Cristòfol and Ramón Marinel.lo. Furthermore, there is a canvas by Le Corbusier, who associated closely with the Barcelona avant-garde circles throughout the 1930s.

36

Joan Miró
Reloj de viento, 1967
(Wind Clock)
Bronze
49.5 x 29.5 x 16 cm
Reg. nº 10541

Alain Jouffroy described this sculpture of Miró's in the following way: "*El reloj de viento*, from 1967, the simplest of all his works, is also the most ambitious. It has the same degree of simplicity as *Mujer y pájaro* ('Woman and Bird'), in which there is a pitchfork and a box. Here too there is an object and a box: a large, country-style spoon. It is at an angle, just like one hand on the face of a clock. Piercing the side, it projects well out of the box, which contains the crown of a hat. Any involvement by the artist is at a minimum – the arrangement of the box on one of its sides, the choice of the central shape, the angle of the spoon, the decision to cast it all in bronze. You may think this is very little. But that little means a great deal. The title, *Reloj de viento* is not only a poetic one. Here the wind changes the symbol of its own reality, its unlimited adventurous character. This piece by Miró stands, then, symbolically, as the instrument which measures the unlimited, the unattainable reality. (...)"

FERRANT

Angel Ferrant

Born in Madrid in 1890, he died there in 1961. An active member of the avant-garde before the Spanish Civil War, he made his first mobiles in 1949. These never included motorised movement, although his interest in movement itself had been evident in all his previous work. He was also interested in "found objects" (wire, cork, shells, stones, metal rods) as items to be included in sculptures or reliefs. With Surrealist aesthetics as his starting point he produced works of two fundamental types: those made of stone, which, as a rule, were figurative; and those of an abstract kind, in which his main interest centred on the inclusion of movement.

37

Angel Ferrant
Mujer hacendosa, 1948
(Hard-working Woman)
Painted wood, string and wire.
145 x 80 x 70 cm
Reg. n° 11989

Of the mobiles made at that time (1949) by Ángel Ferrant, Ricardo Gullón wrote: "In 1948, [Ferrant] was attracted by forms in motion. In the circling of fish, birds, planes, or, more simply, in wind-swept leaves, he discovered a form of beauty capable of expression in sculpture and conceived a large number of objects in which to represent it (...) He wished to dispense with all mechanisms, any kind of mechanical contraption. Thus the movement of the objects would depend only on the objects themselves, and would be produced with a form of freedom giving a sensation of life, imitating life, being its own life."

*T*his room is intended for items in the Museum's holdings that are not regularly exhibited in the Permanent Collection but will be included in monographic or thematic exhibitions temporarily. Holdings from sources other than the Museum but connected in some way with its collections may also be exhibited temporarily in this room.

*T*he Civil War was traumatic at every level of Spanish
society. Where the world of painting and the plastic arts is
concerned, it put paid to the various avant-garde groups which had
sprung up in the Iberian Peninsula during the 20s and 30s. Thus in
the 40s the most urgent task was to restore the Spanish cultural scene.
This initiative found its best examples in certain artists and individual
movements.

In Madrid, Benjamín Palencia attempted to revive the School of
Vallecas. For his part, in 1941 Eugenio D'Ors founded the
Academia Breve de Crítica de Arte which in turn established the
Salones de los Once.

In Barcelona, the most interesting group during these years was Dau
al Set, whose members – painters, critics and poets – worked together
on the extremely interesting publication of the same name.

1948 also saw another initiative worthy of mention – the School of
Altamira, which created a favourable atmosphere for meetings
between members of the younger generations of painters and members
of the surviving pre-war art movements.

One year before, in 1947, the Pórtico group had formed in Saragossa,
sponsored by the bookstore of the same name. Members of this group
produced the first abstract compositions – inspired by the work of Klee,
Miró and Torres García – to appear in post-war Spain.

The surrealist tendencies of the 30s were taken up by another two
groups, the Movimiento Indaliano, and the LADAC group ("The
Archers of Contemporary Art"), one of whose members was Manuel
Millares.

Room 18 offers a view of the new concept of the landscape which
characterised painting and the plastic arts in the post-war period.
Benjamín Palencia became the central figure on the Madrid scene at
that time. Ortega Muñoz's compositions of the fields of Extremadura
also contributed to the development of landscape representation.
Francisco Lozano's work is a fine example of the interpretation of the
Mediterranean landscape. In the mature style of Rafael Zabaleta,

rural themes are predominant. Still life is represented by Luis Castellano. The oils of Pancho Cossío reflect this artist's interest in the materials used in the picture. And Juan Manuel Díaz Caneja devoted himself almost exclusively to the landscape of Castile.

Room 19 contains works by the artists who belonged to the two most important groups in post-war Spain, Pórtico *and* Dau al Set. *Considered as the most active member of the former, the architect Santiago Lagunas produced canvases which can be categorised as fully-fledged examples of abstract art. Eloy Laguardia is another* Portico *member represented in this room; like those of Lagunas, his works reflect the relationship between his group and the* Paris School.

The four principal members of Dau al Set *are also represented in room 19. The paintings of Joan Ponç are full of small, strange beings who occupy areas in which there is no perspective. Modest Cuixart's creations reflect his particular use of psychic Automatism. More closely connected with Dada, Antoni Tàpies's personality as a plastic artist was already clearly defined when he joined the group. Finally, the canvases of Joan Josep Tharrats are an example of the technical processes invented by this painter.*

To illustrate the Pórtico *group's relationship with the abstract art of the* Paris School, *these two rooms (18 and 19) end with a work by Serge Poliakoff. Furthermore, to demonstrate* Dau al Set's *relationship with Surrealist aesthetics, one of the last works exhibited is a canvas by André Masson.*

38

Juan Manuel Díaz Caneja
Paisaje, 1962
(Landscape)
Oil on canvas
97 x 130.7 cm
Reg. n° 01939

In beautiful terms, Gerardo Diego, one of the poets of the
1927 Generation who remained in Spain after the Civil War,
described the pictorial work of Caneja, whose sense of
spirituality Diego linked to the literary tradition of Castile:
"Caneja's painting performs the miracle of bringing together
three virtues very rarely found in one work at the same time
– solidity, nuance and interpretive depth. To combine solidity
of volume with the delicacy of air, the evanescence of
spiritualised colour, is a remarkable accomplishment. When
we step into a room where a solo exhibition of the artist's
work is being held, we suddenly feel the liberating depths of
a great interpreter of earths and skies. Fields of earth,
breasts of air, dreams of sky are superimposed and rest on
a vertical chord, losing themselves in a horizontal melody of
astounding scope and archaic purity. Tierras de Campos for
the poetry of the two Jorges – the one of the dream of
death and the other of the canticle of life. If the river and the
adobe is Jorge Manrique's, then the cube, the almost
mental polyhedron and the obsession with fever – 'Oh,
yellow, yellow' – is Jorge Guillén's."

CANEJA

Juan Manuel Díaz Caneja

*Born in Palencia in 1905, he
died in Madrid in 1988. He
met the sculptor Alberto
Sánchez in Madrid, joining
the* School of Vallecas *with
Alberto himself, Benjamín
Palencia and Maruja Mallo.
In 1929, he moved to Paris,
where he came into contact
with the various avant-garde
movements, particularly
Cubism. In the late 20s and
early 30s, his work
developed towards Cubism,
which was to be the
underlying characteristic of
all his future output. After
the Spanish Civil War, he
concentrated on two subjects
in particular: the* bodegón
*and the Castilian landscape,
always using subdued and
delicate tones.*

3.9

Antoni Tàpies
Personaje, 1950
(Personage)
Mixed media on paper
46 x 54 cm
Reg. n° 11824

On his works of this period, the artist himself made the
following observations: "In those pictures my sensorial
perception paid greater attention to light than colour. As an
example, I could say I left all the background of the picture
dark and there I placed a luminous area like an opening
comparable to a church window. The oil paint produced a
phosphorescent effect. In my later works, light was of
utmost importance as regards the external illumination of
the relief of the textures." *Personaje* retains many of the
characteristic features of the self-portraits that are
numerous in Tàpies's work during this period. In this
composition, as in most of his self-portraits, parts of his
body – his eyes, his eyebrows, his hands – are repeated.
Furthermore, only the top half of the figure is seen and
symbolic elements are included in the composition.

*T*he 1950s was a period of transition in Spanish art. Post-
war isolation and difficulties had not yet come to an end,
but there were certain manifestations which led to considerable
development on the avant-garde scene at the end of the decade and in
the early 60s. It is not possible to speak of one predominant school but
rather of a varied panorama which contained influences from Other
Art and Tachisme and signs of a quest for personal development.
Due to this diversity, the exhibits included here give a view both of
group and individual works dating from this period.

From the realm of the new languages in painting and the plastic arts
are the works of artists such as Salvador Victoria, Manuel Hernández
Mompó and Albert Ràfols Casamada (Room 20). These reflect the
influence of French abstract art. The works of José Guerrero and
Esteban Vicente (Room 21) are those most closely linked to American
Action Painting. Sculpture is represented by the work of Pablo
Serrano (Room 20), who belonged to the El Paso group.

In his works, Salvador Victoria used materials generously, attaching
particular importance to the gesture. Albert Ràfols Casamada moved
away, to a certain extent, from the French informalist approach,
coming closer to American Abstract Expressionism, especially to the
work of painters like Motherwell and Rothko.

Concerned above all with colour and light, in his later years Manuel
Hernández Mompó produced a number of works full of signs which
formed a microcosm all his own.

The works of José Guerrero and Esteban Vicente share the same area.
The style of painting of these two artists, who lived in the United
States, is close to American Abstract Expressionism, although in each
case seen from a personal, very different standpoint.

The works of the Equipo 57 group (Jorge de Oteiza, Pablo Palazuelo,
Eusebio Sempere and Gerardo Rueda) belong to the analytical
tendency in abstract art, which uses formal repertoires stemming from
geometric language. Since its origins, geometric abstraction has been
regarded as a tendency based on reflection and research.

At first deeply influenced by the work of Paul Klee, Pablo Palazuelo (Room 20) soon found his own means of expression in geometric abstraction, and although he too was finally to turn away from it, this movement's hallmark is always evident in his work.

The work of Gerardo Rueda exhibited in Room 20 is a clear example of the artist's preoccupation with spatial organization – possibly inherited from his initial Cubist training. Together with Gustavo Torner and Fernando Zóbel, Rueda played an active part in the creation of the Museo de Arte Abstracto Español in Cuenca.

Eusebio Sempere (Room 23) lived in Paris in the 50s, associating with Arp, Vasarely and Soto. In 1953, he began a series of distinctly abstract works in which a number of geometrical figures stand out usually against black backgrounds. His interest in geometric abstraction was not without a deep sense of lyricism, in which, despite using a different idiom, he coincided with Palazuelo and Rueda.

Oteiza looked especially to Mondrian and Malevich, taking his inspiration, at least at the beginning, from both. Regarding form, he preferred the cube as the basic abstract element for his plastic experimentation. Thanks to a process dubbed by the sculptor himself as desocupación espacial ("spatial deoccupation"), the void became the main element in his work, the dynamic agent which gave meaning to the piece. This can be seen in the group of works exhibited in room 22, which are dedicated entirely to this sculptor, and also in room 20.

Pupils of Jorge de Oteiza, the members of Equipo 57 (Room 20) saw art as a form of behaviour within society and advocated the unification of the arts, an end to the commercial exploitation of the phenomenon of painting and the plastic arts, and pictorial teamwork.

OTEIZA

Jorge de Oteiza

Born in Orio, Guipúzcoa, in 1908. Constantly surrounded by controversy due to his radical, unorthodox views, between 1956 and 1957 he wrote Propósito experimental *("Experimental Purpose"), a book in which he set out his theoretical ideas on experimentation with the void and "spatial deoccupation". He set out on his career as a plastic artist around 1935 with a series of pieces based on found objects. His massive forms with hollow centres dating from around 1950 partially reflect the influence of Henry Moore. In recent years he has turned to experimental Constructivism, thus putting into practice his spatial theories.*

40

Jorge de Oteiza
Caja metafísica, 1958
(Metaphysical Box)
Iron
30 x 32.5 x 30 cm
Reg. n° 08717

Margit Rowell referred to Oteiza's "Metaphysical Boxes" in the following terms: "Oteiza's most prevalent and best-known theme is that of the 'desocupación' of the cube. The works on this theme, conceived and constructed according to the same mathematical and metaphysical premises, appear as a synthesis of all his earlier experiments. The 'Empty Boxes' and 'Metaphysical Boxes', which are formally the most elementary illustrations of this theme, are also the most exemplary. As simple four-sided units or 'boxes', they reflect no ambition on the part of the artist to create 'original' or 'expressive' forms. Yet, despite the avowed attempt to express universal laws, these works – in their multiple variations – are neither neutral, anonymous, nor impersonal."

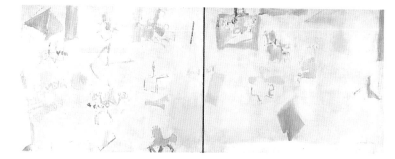

41

Manuel Mompó
Composición, 1966
(Composition)
Oil on canvas
114 x 293 cm
Reg. n° 04744

Colour, light and a mysterious microcosm of undecipherable signs are found in the work of Mompó, as in the case of *Composición*. José Corredor-Matheos analyzed this phenomenon: (...) "We know that reality as it normally appears to us is the invention of our senses. Here, the artist is captivated by lights, the reverberation of colours, the brilliance of blots and lines. It is the crackling of fire, the result of throwing the possible light on the spectacle of everyday life. The Impressionists cleared the way and it may be a cliché – but what does that matter? – to recall the importance of light on the shores of Mompó's Mediterranean. Light illuminates as much as it veils: a mist prevents us, by the side of that mythical sea, from seeing too much. The painter knows that seeing too much prevents us from distinguishing what matters and so paints with his eyes half-closed. To appreciate the result we have to open ours wide. The light is on the verge of leaving the canvas blank – the ultimate aim – or perhaps Mompó has achieved, conceptually speaking, 'white on white', and, now returning, allows those strange, extremely light creatures to flap their wings."

HERNÁNDEZ MOMPÓ

Manuel Hernández
Mompó

Born in Valencia in 1927, he died in Madrid in 1992. In 1951, he travelled to Paris, where he first came into contact with the avant-garde art movements. After continuing his pictorial training in Italy and Holland, in 1968 he made a group of large-format works for the Venice Biennale which won him the Unesco Prize. His work, which can be categorised as belonging to a particular kind of informalism, began with urban landscapes and themes, but gradually developed as a plastic universe full of lyricism in which colour played an extremely important part.

42

José Guerrero
Composición, 1956
(Composition)
Oil on canvas
194.5 x 129.5 cm
Reg. n° 02546

GUERRERO

José Guerrero

Born in Granada in 1914, he died in Barcelona in 1991. He settled in Paris but in 1949 moved to New York, where he came into contact with the most prominent figures of Abstract Expressionism – Rothko, Motherwell, Pollock and Kline – with whom he took part in various group exhibitions. He returned to Spain in the 80s. Having abandoned his initial figurative style, he embarked upon what was to become his greatest achievement – a series of works incorporating the approach of American Action Painting and a "cult" to light and colour closely related to the sensibility of his Andalusian and Mediterranean origins.

The skill with which José Guerrero brings together the teachings of Abstract Expressionism and memories of his homeland in the pictures from this time – as in *Composición* – is described in the following reflections by Francisco Calvo Serraller: ... "Whatever Guerrero's personal reasons for going to America and settling in New York, it is certain that when he arrived he found the eruption of American Abstract Expressionism in full swing and realised how extraordinarily important it was. By 1953, scarcely three years after his arrival, Guerrero was putting his signature to pictures in which he had set out on that path. It was not, however, until the second half of the 50s that his most personal stylistic features became clearly recognisable, including those which revealed his Mediterranean European connections, not to mention his most quaintly racial anthropological clichés, such as those deriving from his decidedly Andalusian roots. This meant not only his burgeoning sense of colour, but also his instinctive use of ever warmer and more luminous colours. In this sense, I am not surprised that the American critics referred – quite rightly – to his Spanish sensitivity."

Esteban Vicente
Medio Oeste, 1953
(Midwest)
Oil on canvas
122 x 91.5 cm
Reg. n° 10621

Esteban Vicente made the following observations on his own painting: "To begin with, I use a very limited palette. I don't use earthy colours. I obtain these by mixing the primaries. Earthy colours are very beautiful, but very hard to use. When they come straight out of the tube they're too dark. Mixing them, I get the brightness I want. For example, with green, orange and a small amount of red I get a bright ochre. When I start painting a picture I work with very thin paint. After that I don't use any other medium. I work with the paint for a long time and little by little it gets thicker. It has to be like that to achieve the desired effect. I try to avoid thick brush-strokes and so use a brush with very soft bristles. If I change anything, I do it by scraping, since I always work with fresh paint."

VICENTE

Esteban Vicente

Born in Turégano, Segovia, in 1903. Having been a member of the Republican government during the Spanish Civil War, he took up residence in the United States in 1936, *where he came into contact with the main exponents of the New York School, including Jackson Pollock, Mark Rothko and Willem de Kooning, and shared a studio with de Kooning from 1950 on. Virtually unknown in Spain until the 80s, his work can be categorised as belonging* *to American Action Painting. During the 50s his compositions basically concentrated on the juxtaposition of warm and cool colours at times arranged through geometrical shapes. His latest canvases have been compared by some critics to the work of Rothko.*

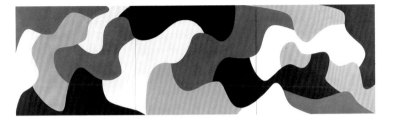

EQUIPO 57

Juan Cuenca, Ángel Duarte, José Duarte, Agustín Ibarrola y Juan Serrano

44

Equipo 57
Tríptico, 1960
(Triptych)
Acrylic on hardboard
122 x 411 cm
Reg. nº 01854

According to Ángel Llorente Hernández, one of the most competent experts on *Equipo 57*, this group's work went through four different stages. In the first, the composition is based on a form of geometry in which a preponderance of straight lines separate the different areas of colour, while in the next – a period of transition – there is an obvious tendency towards curved surfaces. In the third stage, there is a certain serialism in both colour and form which, furthermore, begin to become smaller. Finally, the group's later works have certain things in common with optical kinetic art.

Tríptico might well be said to belong to the third stage, by which time the outlines delimiting the various coloured surfaces are softer while the motifs are smaller and repeated with a certain rhythm. Also noteworthy is the format of this picture – one of the group's largest – as well as the fact that the tones are grey and black only. Both things – the monumental, rectangular format and the use of *grisaille* for the composition – could well be an indirect tribute to Picasso's *Guernica*.

Juan Cuenca was born in Puente Genil, Córdoba, in 1934, Ángel Duarte in Aldeanueva del Camino, Cáceres, in 1930, José Duarte in Córdoba in 1928, Agustín Ibarrola in Bilbao in 1930, and Juan Serrano in Córdoba in 1929. Equipo 57 made their début in the summer of 1957 with the techniques of the sculptor Jorge de Oteiza as their inspiration. The group's works are inseparable from their theoretical research, which comes together in a number of writings under the title Manifiesto sobre la interactividad del espacio plástico *("Manifesto on the Interactivity of Plastic Space"). Their pictorial work, which has always been based on constructive abstraction, developed in four stages, the last of which reflects a certain concomitance with optical and kinetic art.*

PALAZUELO

Pablo Palazuelo

*Born in Madrid, in 1916.
Having studied at Oxford, in
1948 he moved to Paris,
where most of his
development as a painter and
plastic artist took place. His
first works date from 1940, a
time when he was influenced
by Neo-Cubism and the work
of Klee, Mondrian and
Kandinsky. After 1946, his
work became clearly abstract
and can be categorised as
Constructivist. His first three-
dimensional pieces, to which
he transferred his previous
research work with canvas,
date from 1954.*

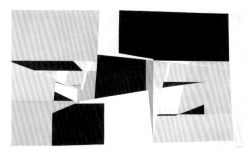

45

Pablo Palazuelo
Otoños, 1952
(Autumns)
Oil on canvas
82 x 143 cm
Reg. n° 08115

In an exchange of writings between Claude Esteban and
Pablo Palazuelo, the former referred to the painter's stylistic
development from the time of his first works by describing
imaginary compositions very close to the formal conception
of *Otoños*: "I look at the first drawings of yours I ever saw,
some of the oils from the 40s which I have been able to see
reproduced. Of the 'real' that was, in effect, affirmed and
acknowledged, there remains only a network of lines – a
kind of spread-out spatial configuration in which without a
shadow of a doubt something of the Cubist preoccupation
with the outlines of the object and its two-dimensional
representation on the cloth could be discerned. But we can
go no further in our comparison. While the Cubist
deliberately locks himself up in a kind of mental cell where
objects stifle space, as it were, I see you throwing open the
windows of that confined place and giving the lines that
power of expansion, those virtualities of irradiation that
reject closed forms..."

*D*ue to the complexity of the development of Spanish and
international art in the 40s and 50s, there are various
routes for viewing the works exhibited in these rooms. The following
route is only a suggestion for one of the various ways of viewing the
development of Spanish art and its context as the visitor may opt for
either the development of Spanish art or that of its contexts.

24-26   CONTEXTS OF SPANISH ART

*S*panish artists got to know about European and American art
through trips, exhibitions, magazines and publications of all kinds.
Room 24 contains various key examples of the works they saw. First of
all, there are pieces by Asger Jorn and Pierre Alechinsky. These are
followed, in the second area of Room 24, by examples of the work of
Graham Sutherland, Francis Bacon and Henry Moore. Rooms 25 and
26 contain major pieces by Yves Klein and Lucio Fontana.
The Cobra group first made its appearance in November 1948, its
principal members being Asger Jorn, Karel Appel, Constant and
Corneille. The name comes from the initials of the cities of origin of the
various members – Copenhagen, Brussels and Amsterdam. The works
by Pierre Alechinsky and Asger Jorn exhibited in these rooms are
examples of an Expressionist type of figurativeness which, to a certain
extent, link up with the pictorial world of Spain's Antonio Saura.
Representation of the English artists who influenced the development
of European art in the second half of this century begins with the
work of Graham Sutherland, who initially drew his inspiration from
organic growth, with which he attempted to capture the essence of the
human form.
Another key figure in contemporary British art was Francis Bacon,
who submitted the figures in his pictures to metamorphoses in which

*specific features become blurred and individual miseries become
tragedies common to all mankind.*

*The last great British artist represented in this room is Henry Moore,
an extremely important figure from the world of sculpture in the
second half of the century.*

*Room 25 is an invitation to see the work of Yves Klein, who in the
late 40s began working with pure colours and in 1955 exhibited a
series of monochrome works in Paris, although his preference for blue
led to his name being associated with this colour (which he used as a
means of evocation). The artist himself called this ultramarine blue
I.K.B ("International Klein Blue") and, according to the critics, it
represented the expression of "the undefinable and the immaterial".
Lucio Fontana, who devised the theory of what he called "Spatialism"
is represented in a major set of works (Room 26). Fontana's great
preoccupation with seeking out a synthesis of all the physical elements
in artistic creation – "colour, sound, movement, space, in a unity that
was both ideal and material" – and his deep desire to do away with
the limits dividing painting and sculpture is evident in the works
exhibited in this room. As a whole these compositions with their
monochrome or perforated surfaces produce a kind of peculiar,
enveloping atmosphere in which the spectator ceases to be an observer
and feels that he or she is part of the work and has become immersed
in the magical space created by it.*

Born in Dublin in 1909, he died in Madrid in 1992. A self-taught artist, between 1927 and 1928 he travelled to Berlin and Paris. Having returned to London, he held an exhibition of furniture, paintings and gouaches at his Queensbury Mews studio, although after 1931 he gradually abandoned decoration to dedicate himself to painting. In 1944, after destroying all his previous canvases he took up painting again. Bacon's work, which can be categorised as belonging to the European figurative art of the 60s, depicts with tragic overtones the solitude and angst of an isolated and vulnerable modern-day man in a hostile society.

Francis Bacon
Figura tumbada, 1966
(Reclining Figure)
Oil on canvas
198 x 147 cm
Reg. n° 08088

Bacon's work prompted Michel Leiris to make the following observation: (...) "Generally closed and exiguous, the space of the picture – a medium which is neither a substitute nor a scaled-down model but rather a replica of our own – becomes, whether in the case of an impersonal room or, when larger, of an open space as vulgar as one wishes, a kind of box in which, ideally, the spectator is fictionally situated in the same place as that in which – apparently on his same scale – the thing is shown to him; thus rewarded with a role less insignificant than that of an observer chained to an armchair, he is promoted to the position of a *voyeur* who is present in person at the scenic fiction with no narratable anecdote offered him and is caught in the trap of a space almost always closed in on itself but always open to whoever has the imagination to penetrate it – which is what the whole contrivance seems to invite him to do."

47

Yves Klein
Antropometría sin título (ANT 56), 1960
[Untitled Anthropometry (ANT 56)]
Dry pigment on synthetic resin on paper
glued to canvas
78.5 x 279 cm
Reg. n° 12145

KLEIN

Yves Klein

In March 1960, Klein gave a live performance in painting at
the *Galerie International d'Art Contemporain* in Paris using
the so-called *living brush* process, in which three models
covered in paint dragged themselves over or crept on all
fours across the paper and the cloth while the artist himself
directed their movements. Klein later declared: "My models
became living paintbrushes!

"I had rejected the paintbrush long before. It was too
psychological. I painted with a roller, which is more
anonymous, attempting to create a 'distance' – at least an
intellectual distance, without variations – between the
canvas and myself during the work. Now, like a miracle, the
paintbrush was returning, but this time with a life of its own.
At my direction the flesh itself applied the colour to the
surface, and with perfect exactness. I was able to stand all
the time at a distance of 'x' from my canvas and in this way
control my creation throughout its execution.

"In this way I stayed clean. I didn't get the colour all over
myself, not even on my fingertips. The work finished itself
before me, at my direction with the complete collaboration
of the model. And I was able to celebrate its birth into the
tangible world in a fitting manner, in evening dress...

"Through this demonstration – or rather this technique – I
particularly wanted to tear down the temple veil of the
studio. [I did not want] to keep any of my process hidden."

Born in Nice, France, in
1928, he died in Paris in
1962. In Paris he worked in
a variety of jobs. In 1952, he
travelled to Japan, after
which his works were deeply
influenced by Oriental
culture. From the very
beginning he used pure
colours in his paintings, but
the colour that is most closely
identified with his work is
ultramarine blue, known as
I.K.B. ("International Klein
Blue"). In 1960, he founded
the Les Nouveaux
Réalistes *movement with*
Pierre Restany. Klein's
output includes painting,
sculpture, "performances",
architectural projects and
writing, which demonstrates
not only his treatment of the
widest variety of techniques
but also his personal view of
the nature of art.

FONTANA

Lucio Fontana

Born in Rosario de Santa Fe, Argentina, in 1899, he died in Comabbio, Italy, in 1968. In 1934, he became a member of the "Italian Abstract" group of artists and in 1935 joined another avant-garde group, Abstraction-Création, *in Paris. That same year he added his signature to the manifesto for* Arte Astratta Italiana's *first group exhibition. From 1947, he drafted the group's series of "Special Manifestos". His early sculptures display the influence of Alexandre Archipenko. However, in his later years his main preoccupation was with the inclusion of three-dimensional space in the picture, which he achieved by puncturing and tearing the bare, pigment-free canvas.*

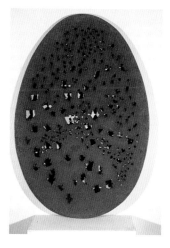

48

Lucio Fontana
*Concepto espacial.
El fin de Dios*, 1963
*(Spatial Conception.
The End of God)*
Mixed media on
canvas
178 x 123 cm
Reg. n° 11744

Giulio Carlo Argue spoke in the following terms of Lucio Fontana's work, particularly the canvases which, like this one, belong to the *Spatial Conception* series: ..."For Fontana the concrete definition of space was the true theoretical object of art. With him space was a fixation – although a lucid and obsessive one. Thus, he structured his theory of art as a theory of space, giving the name 'Spatialism' to the movement which, when no longer a young man, he had created in 1947 and was followed by the youngest and most brilliant artists in Milan. Many of his works from that period are entitled 'Spatial Conception'. He maintained that the conception of space in art should adapt to the most modern scientific thought, to Einstein in particular, although within another, very different, order as it cannot be defined in numbers or formulae, but only through art in the plastic and colouristic intensity of its fragments of intrinsically spatial matter. For him space was reality in a pure and absolute statë, standing apart from the multiplicity of things through its greatness, its weight, its easy adaptation to the quantitative adjustment of light. In turn, the amount of the space invented was pure quality; and colour also – which in empirical reality was quantity and relationship – thus became an absolute quality..."

27-29   IMAGES OF INFORMALISM

Informalism describes a type of painting, both figurative and non-figurative, in which both the gesture and the action are basic ingredients. The term is used here only as a reference and does not imply homogeneity, as the concept encompasses the work of a wide variety of artists.

In Spain, informalism developed mainly in two places – Madrid and Catalonia – and it was in Barcelona where works of this type, in which Antoni Tàpies was considered the pioneer, first appeared.

In Madrid, the focus of the various directions taken by informalism lay in the El Paso *group, founded in February 1957. Just as El Paso made its appearance, other painters and sculptors were beginning to take an interest in this tendency, some being members of the "Cuenca Group", so called because they took part in the founding of the* Museo de Arte Abstracto Español *in Cuenca in 1966. Works by members of this group and by* El Paso's *main followers are exhibited in Room 27 next to others by artists who chose their own paths in informalism. An interest in the material used was an underlying factor in the work of Martín Chirino at this time. The purity of his lines, the austerity of his media and a sense of the lyrical are other constant factors.*

Into his works of that time that are exhibited in this room, Rafael Canogar poured all the expressive energy that is characteristic of him, demonstrating his exceptional command of materials.

Despite a sober palette, the works of Manuel Viola, who at first turned to poetry, are always full of bold gestures. His pictures are the result of surrealist tendencies influenced by French Tachisme.

The works of Luis Feito which date from this time reflect strong colour contrasts heralding the explosions of colour typical of his pictures of the late 60s.

From the very beginning, Lucio Muñoz and Josep Guinovart displayed a profound interest in the materials used in their works. Guinovart's predilection for Benjamín Palencia's "matter" pictures reflect this Catalan artist's attraction to unusual pictorial methods. Around 1955, Lucio Muñoz began to use wood in his works, finally allowing it to take over not only the surface of the work but also the very support, giving it an extremely original appearance.

Francisco Farreras, another of the artists represented in this room, displays the same interest in his materials. He included different types of sand in his mid-50s works before changing to tissue-paper collages *around the end of that decade.*

Also more inclined to explore the secrets of the material than those of the gesture, Gustavo Torner is an artist who worked alone, although he associated with and took an active part in the founding of the Museo de Arte Abstracto Español *in Cuenca.*

The production of Fernando Zóbel (from the Philippines) has little in common with that of the previous artists, his work being rather the result of a combination of the poetic art of Action Painting and Oriental aesthetic ideas.

The work of Manuel Millares and Manuel Rivera – like most of the artists included in these rooms, members of the El Paso group – is exhibited in Room 28. Manuel Millares began using burlap as the main component in his works around 1953. Colour – or rather the almost complete lack of it – is another constant feature of his later style, which contributes to the general sensation of a deeply dramatic character in his works.

But perhaps one of the artists who extols the virtues of that great central issue of informalism – the material – in the most original way is Manuel Rivera, who explored the play of light produced by metal fabric, a material which was to become the most prominent feature of his works.

Antonio Saura (Room 29) uses a violent, gestural language always midway between the abstract and the figurative. He has concentrated not only on stereotypes from the political and cultural history of Spain but also on the most typical symbols of the consumer society, inverting our usual way of seeing them.

(49)

Manuel Millares
Cuadro 173, 1962
(Picture 173)
Mixed media on burlap
130 x 163 cm
Reg. n° 10583

Millares's "blood-stained burlaps" inspired Rafael Alberti to write the following poem in Rome in 1965:

In Rome or in Paris,
New York, Buenos Aires, Madrid, Calcutta, Cairo ...
in yet more places,
there are torn burlaps,
worn-out shoes stuck to the bone,
stumps, hard remains,
charred refuse,
deep pits, dry
worlds of bygone rust,
of clotted blood,
human skin, eaten away like dead lava,
gnawn and tragic, signs that accuse, cry out,
though they have no mouth,
grating shrieks that wound
as much as silence.
From where this refuse,
these one-armed landslides,
holes about to be made yet bigger
slow strips of torn weft,
curdled jumbles, clouds of chalk,
bright reds, from where?
What will spring out from here, what will happen?
what will burst out from these violent scarecrows,
what will tumble out of this blind, tattered skin
when it breaks its threads, when it suddenly makes
its opened seams bite, when it illuminates its blackness,
its trifles and its calciums with an overwhelming radiance
capable of giving birth to the very newest beauty? (...)

MILLARES

Manuel Millares

Born in Las Palmas de Gran Canaria in 1926, he died in Madrid in 1972. In 1950, he was a founder member of the LADAC *("The Archers of Contemporary Art") group. In 1957, he took part in the founding and development of the* El Paso *group. One year later, in 1958, his article "El homúnculo en la pintura actual" ("The Homunculus in Present-day Painting") was published in the issue of the magazine* Papeles de Son Armadans *dedicated to the* El Paso *group. His first works, the famous* pictografías canarias *("Canarian Pictographs"), were influenced by the study of the Guanche culture. He subsequently became interested in surfaces and textures – leading to his mature style – although he never strayed from the limits of informalism.*

50

Antonio Saura
Grito n° 7, 1959
(Shout n° 7)
Oil on canvas
250 x 200 cm
Reg. n° D-0036

SAURA

Antonio Saura

Born in Huesca, in 1930. In 1953, he travelled to Paris, where he stayed until 1955 and for some time took part in the activities of the Surrealist group. In 1957, having returned to Madrid, he made a decisive contribution to the creation of the El Paso *group, a veritable melting pot for renovation in informalism through the incorporation of the gestural techniques used on the international art scene. Beginning with a period greatly influenced by Surrealism, his work later turned towards an expressionist type of informalism, with compositions generally based on black and white tones which suggested the influence of the great Classical masters like Rembrandt, Goya and El Greco.*

Saura's palette and his way of working were accurately described by Juan Eduardo Cirlot, when he referred to pictures in the style and from the period we are dealing with: "Figurativeness – reduced to a state of turbulent, hectic and demoniacal appearances – and abstraction – especially sensitised by the use of brush-strokes in great, swift trails that suggest nothing corporeal – join together so intimately in Saura's works that it is often difficult to see whether they fit into one field or another. Truly his art is the suture of opposite worlds, hence the depth of this clamour and its echoes. As in the black and the white, in the movement and the stillness of the two dimensions, life and death intertwine and fuse their contradictory qualities. (...) Grey appears between black and white to carry out necessary transitions. The brush-strokes or the strokes of the impasto or the palette knife, or the gestures cruelly drawn with the wooden part of the paintbrush, whirl and confuse the spiral with the broken, with the choking in syncopes. In some works the particular mobility of all these elements is as if neutralized and a kind of immobility is generated that is different from stillness, similar to that apparent serenity which is jolted internally by forces that attempt to uproot it."

30   JEAN DUBUFFET

The creator of Art Brut, *Jean Dubuffet is a key figure*
within the context of European art after World War II.
His work brings together the main characteristics of
a response to the situation of those times and conveys
a rejection of the cruelty and misery of the War. In the
late 40s, he produced a series of compositions based on
a compact material to which he added sand, ash, tar, etc.,
making slashes in the form of lines which suggest
strange motifs.

Together with the works of Dubuffet exhibited in this room,
there are two small compositions by America's Mark Tobey,
thus suggesting the relationship that existed between the
European and American tendencies and at the same time
demonstrating this artist's knowledge and study of Oriental
calligraphy.

Also included in this area is a work by Yves Klein taken from
his so-called "Fire" paintings series which acts as a
complement to Dubuffet's and Tobey's works.

51

Jean Dubuffet
Suelo terroso, 1957
(Earthy Ground)
Oil on canvas
73 x 92 cm
Reg. n° 12092

DUBUFFET
....
Jean Dubuffet

*Born in Le Havre,
France, in 1901, he died
in Paris in 1985. In
1944, he held his first
one-man exhibition at
the René Drouin
Gallery in Paris. In the
40s, he began his
figurative works,
including innovative
elements in his paintings
such as graffiti,
drawings, marks and
incisions made through
automatic drawing
techniques. This method
plus the importance he
attached to the treatment
of the material was to
culminate in the
Materiologies (1950-60)
and Texturologies
(1957-58) series. In
1962, he began the
L'Hourloupe series,
which he continued to
work on until 1974. In
these pictures he used a
limited number of pure
colours painted on
curvilinear, interlacing
segments which extended
over the whole surface of
the picture.*

Of other works of his similar to this one, Jean Dubuffet said the following: "Perhaps I am not the only one to love the ground so much. Perhaps all of us – and much more than we might think – are very fond of things like this without realising it. In which direction does our gaze usually turn when we are not controlling it? Compared with a single instant when we fix our gaze on an object and are fully aware that we are doing so, how many hours a day are our eyes busy without us knowing it? (...)
"Notice that my predilection is not for picturesque, luxuriously polished or adorned floors, exceptional floors that attract one's attention. By no means!... I don't like exceptional things; what beguiles me most is the ordinary, the banal (...) For me a street devoid of any special details or features, a dirty wooden floor, a piece of bare dusty earth which it would not cross anyone's mind to look at – at least on purpose (and let alone to paint) – are sources of intoxication and exhilaration.(...)"

31   THE SPANISH REALISTS

The group known as Realismo madrileño *("Madrid Realism")
was formed by a number of painters and plastic artists whose mature
work appeared in the 60s. The members live in Madrid and the
painter Antonio López García is its central figure. Together with the
representatives of informalism – and despite their obvious differences –
the artists belonging to this group moved in the same circles and took
part in the same events which led to the renewal of the art scene in
the 60s and 70s.*

*In his oil paintings Antonio López García depicts the themes of
everyday life with great technical precision. His interest centres on
intimist scenes portraying the fabric of urban life in Madrid through
magnificent perspectives in rectangular pictures that are all very
similar in size.*

*One of the favourite subjects of the sculptor Francisco López
Hernández is the human figure, which he almost always reproduces
life-size in his work. Another facet of his work is the representation of
commonplace objects, usually in small pieces and in relief.*

Xavier Valls, a painter having little to do with Realismo madrileño*,
has spent most of his career in Paris. According to Valls himself, his
oils depict life by divesting it of the anecdotal in order to reduce it to
the essential.*

LÓPEZ GARCÍA

Antonio López García

Born in Tomelloso, Ciudad Real, in 1936. He received his initial training from his uncle, the painter Antonio López Torres. In 1949, he moved to Madrid to study at the Escuela de Bellas Artes de San Fernando, *completing his studies in 1955. He was a key figure in the group known as the "Madrid Realists", and despite portraying the everyday in both his pictures and sculptures, he never ignored the darker aspects of a universe at times magical and always filled with silent objects. His commonest themes include interiors and urban landscapes. Also characteristic of López García's style are perspective, which is sometimes distorted, and his meticulous execution. He recently became a member of the Royal San Fernando Academy of Art.*

52

Antonio López García
***Madrid visto desde el Cerro del Tío Pío*, 1962-63
*(Madrid from Cerro del Tío Pío)***
Oil on panel
102 x 129.5 cm
Reg. n° DE-0508

The city of Madrid which Antonio López – as he himself admits – depicts from different angles, is one of the painter's favourite subjects: "I have worked on three very clearly defined views of the city: from a high place – a balcony or a window – in large paintings with the sea of houses merging with the horizon; from the outskirts with the city in the background; and from the street." His canvas *Madrid visto desde el Cerro del Tío Pío* is a fine example of the view of the city from the outskirts, and like his other work in this room, *Madrid desde Capitán Haya* ("Madrid from Capitán Haya Street") portrays a Madrid street without people or cars. This is always the case with López's painting, for, as he himself says, he can only paint the permanent aspects of reality. An essential ingredient in his paintings is light, and the artist once said: (...) "It's hard to realise, but the light in the countryside makes me marvel. The landscape can be depicted in a relief, but light, the seductiveness of light – its greatest attraction and what gives it character – can only be captured in the most immediate and expressive way through painting."

32 EDUARDO CHILLIDA

Eduardo Chillida is a central figure in the world of Spanish and international sculpture. In the early 50s, his style developed towards a form of abstract art which stressed the importance of the materials and techniques used and the symbolic value of the motif.

All the materials chosen by Chillida possess a strength which gives rise to the form and poetry of each sculpture. Thus, in the case of alabaster that strength is light and its transparency is the most important feature of the work. In the case of wood, it is the trunk with all its knots and rough features that the sculptor deliberately includes in his work. With iron his awareness of the material results in it becoming an essential element of expression. In the case of steel and reinforced concrete, density and gravity become the basic components of a highly monumental type of sculpture. Chillida is aware of each material and its peculiarities, he boosts its potential and places it at the disposal of the essential elements in his poetic style.

CHILLIDA

Eduardo Chillida

Born in San Sebastián in 1924. Since 1958, the date of his first one-man exhibition at the Clan gallery in Madrid, Chillida's work has been exhibited all over the world and is represented in major museums, including the New York Guggenheim. His sculptures began with a series of figurative pieces which, at a very early stage (around 1950) were replaced by abstract works. Whether modelled through dynamic strokes or as heavy architectonic masses, his favourite materials are concrete, steel, alabaster and, above all, iron. Chillida has also produced major works in the fields of engraving and printing.

53

Eduardo Chillida
El espíritu de los pájaros I, 1952
(The Spirit of the Birds I)
Wrought iron and stone
56 x 92.5 x 42.5 cm
Reg. n° 01337

Eduardo Chillida made his first iron sculpture in 1951 – a piece entitled *Illarik* ("Stele"). Although he has never actually stopped using iron, from then on and until 1960 it was to be his favourite material. Inspired by sculptures such as *El espíritu de los pájaros*, Octavio Paz wrote:

…"Between 1952 and 1956 Chillida produced a number of sculptures in which iron, sometimes with pebbles and stones from rivers, was honed and sharpened in slender jets which curved or leapt out onto the asphalt of space. At one extreme these works are close to cruel sexuality and, at the other, winged elegance. The keen, the sharp, the penetrating and the puncturing, that which skewers, sticks into, perforates, and at the same time flies, undulates, whirls round, meanders, flutters, winds – the beak and the wing, talons and feathers. Birds but also sects, arrows, javelins, the zig-zag of electrical current. How can one not think of the tribes with fantastic spears and assegais that are drawn on a page with the ink of Kufic script? Except that Chillida's page is the open air. The flight of spears and feathers, black and blue flight: iron and wind."

33   MARIO MERZ, JANNIS KOUNELLIS AND PIER PAOLO CALZOLARI

*K*nown above all as exponents of Art Povera, *Merz, Kounellis and Calzolari can be considered classical artists. "Art Povera," says Mario Merz, "is important because it is linked to life (...) [In it] is the idea that it is necessary to use anything whatsoever from life in art, not to reject things because one thinks that life and art are mutually exclusive."*

The materials most commonly used by Mario Merz in his work are stone, earth, wood, metal and glass, and also objects of the same kind together, such as bundles of firewood, bits of fruit, even piles of newspapers. 1974 saw the beginning of a series of major pictorial works in which he included the same elements as those he had used previously.

Jannis Kounellis uses a wide variety of objects and materials, very often objets trouvés, *to display the elementary force of living things. As a complement he also uses the colour black, light and various other elements which, in many cases, act as a reference to death.*

In his works, Pier Paolo Calzolari uses such unusual materials as tobacco leaves, frozen structures, fire, surfaces of salt, moss, grass, honey and foam, neon inscriptions, felt, lead and tin, as he believes that the greater the material's physical purity and potential for transmutation, the more valid it is.

Between rooms 33 – Art Povera *– and 36 –* Pop Art *– stands a piece by Michelangelo Pistoletto. It has not been placed there by chance, for it is by an artist whose work at first belonged to* Art Povera *but whose standpoint has developed and at times comes close to* Pop Art.

54 ....

Mario Merz
El atardecer en la tacita, 1979
(Dusk in the Demitasse)
Acrylic and neon on canvas
410 x 283 cm
Reg. n° 08741

This canvas features the numeric progression in neon
found in many of Merz's sculptures from the 70s that
are a mathematical transposition of the theme of the
spiral and the concept of time and creation. On the
meaning of Fibonacci's numeric sequence (which is
used here), the artist said the following to Suzanne
Pagé and Jean-Christophe Ammann, thus providing us
with essential information on the meaning of this
painting: "Fibonacci's sequence corresponds to a
mathematical arrangement in spiral form that is different
from Renaissance perspective and is also organic.
Fibonacci made experimentation with reproduction in
rabbits the starting point of his studies. I thought it
would be interesting for art to arrange numbers in
space following his progression. In nature a kind of
predisposition to asymmetry exists which is produced
by nature itself. Symmetry leads to a closing-in on
itself. Asymmetry should mean a going out, which is
why the asymmetry of Fibonacci's numeric sequence
fascinated me. The spiral is a symbol of time, it is
expansion from the centre to the periphery. But the
expansion of space corresponds to the concept of time
itself (...) The spiral is thus an organic form which to my
mind should always necessarily follow the organic
rhythm of the hand that created it. My idea is closer to
Pollock than to Renaissance perspective. The true
spiral turns around itself, just like Dervishes dancing.
The world turns as they do, starting from the periphery
and moving towards the centre. Moving from a fixed
point towards the centre is a completely different idea
which comes from the Renaissance and perspective.
For example, I have often punctured a piece of cloth
with a neon light because for me puncturing a painted
piece of cloth produced an interesting contrast, like two
different periods crossing or intersecting."

M E R Z   ....

Mario Merz

Born in Milan, Italy, in
1925. He began to paint in
the 1950s, holding his first
one-man exhibition in 1954.
Considered one of the most
important promoters of Art
Povera, *around 1967 he*
began to use neon and make
his characteristic igloo-
shaped structures. In the 70s,
he introduced new elements,
such as newspapers,
numbers and animal figures,
into his work. In 1974, he
returned to painting,
including elements from his
previous work in his
pictures. In 1982, his work
was included at the Kassel
Dokumenta.

34-35   ANTONI TÀPIES

Rooms 34 and 35 give an insight into the works of Antoni Tàpies. They can be viewed either as part of the chronological development of Spanish art or within the context of their relationship to international art, itself strongly influenced by this Catalan artist.

Originally a member of Dau al Set, *Tàpies developed his own form of Surrealism. Subsequently, and until around 1963 the material he used in each work was the most important feature.*

In the late 60s and early 70s, this artist became interested in everyday objects as a source of artistic inspiration. His work reflects a predilection for the humblest of materials, which in general are similar to those used by Art Povera.

In the 80s, the experts noticed a return to the "pictorial" in his work. In his pictures the material became more fluid, transparencies were used, and his colour was more luminous.

Tàpies has never ceased to take an interest in every field of artistic creation – painting, sculpture, engraving, writing and scenography.

55

Antoni Tàpies
Superposición de materia gris, 1961
(Superimposition of Grey Matter)
Mixed media on canvas
197 x 263 cm
Reg. n° 10532

The painstaking method used by Tàpies to make his "matter" works, one example being *Superposición de materia gris*, has been described in detail by Manuel J. Borja-Villel: "The technical process through which Tàpies creates his 'matter' paintings expresses the notion of the formless. First he applies a coat of varnish to the cloth and before it dries he sifts powdered marble, sand or other materials and pigments over it. Then he adds paint with a thick brush or a paintbrush to different areas to create a figure, an object or a field of colour. Once the top layers have been applied the material begins to crack, revealing its structural components. Sometimes the artist emphasises this by peeling off pieces. The splits and cracks and the different colours and textures do not necessarily follow the lines of a figure or object whose inflections relate to the material and the object represented. In this way the distinction between the figure 'with form' and the 'formless' space which surrounds it becomes confused."

TÀPIES

Antoni Tàpies

Born in Barcelona, in 1923. In 1948, he founded the Dau al Set *group and magazine with Joan Brossa, later being joined by Cuixart, Tharrats, Ponç and Arnau Puig. In 1970, he made his first sculptures. His early work displayed Surrealist aesthetics but developed into a special type of informalism in which matter, monochrome and* sgraffito *took on special importance, all connected in a certain manner with* Zen *philosophy. Winner of a number of the most important international prizes, his work has been acknowledged in exhibitions organised by some of the most prestigious museums in the world. He has also made successful incursions into literature, having published* La pràctica de l'art *(1970),* Cartes per a la Teresa *(1974) and* Memòria personal *(1978).*

*T*he diversity of Spanish and international art in the 50s
and 60s found in abstract art, Pop Art *and figurative*
narration, directions whose definition is extremely complex. For
example, in Room 36 the works of the sculptor Andreu Alfaro and the
painter Joan Hernández Pijuan are both abstract but are very
different from one another.

Alfaro was a member of the Parpalló *group, which was formed*
in 1956. In the 70s, he worked with bars and pipes made from
industrial materials. The forms in his 80s works are greatly
simplified.

In the same room there is one of Joan Hernández Pijuan's
latest works. This artist's style was at first informalist but
developed towards an evaluation of space and the application
of the stroke.

Room 36 contains other works which, although different, are
nevertheless related. The piece by Alfredo Alcaín is a good example
of the type of Pop Art *which dispensed with emphasis and came*
closer to a certain degree to pictorial precepts. In contrast is a
painting by Luis Gordillo. Finally there is a large painting by
Philip Guston which displays not only an original form of figurative
narration but also an extremely innovative pictorial approach.

Room 36 might be regarded as an antechamber to Rooms 37 and 38,
which contain exceptional examples of Pop Art *and figurative*
narration in Spain.

Equipo Crónica *(Room 37) was a group formed in Valencia in 1964 who worked together until the death of Rafael Solbes in 1981. In the early years, when their works revolved around different thematic series,* Equipo Crónica *dealt with the imagery created by the mass media using it with a strong measure of social criticism. Other series dealt with the artist's role in the creative process and analyzed art in relation to its environment.*

Eduardo Arroyo (Room 38) uses figurativeness with a vigorous, artistic approach committed to Spanish life, to which he makes constant allusions in his work. His deep, ironic criticism of political and social systems is characteristic of all his work as an artist, as is his demythologizing treatment of historical figures.

In the 60s, Luis Gordillo based his iconography (Room 39) on images from advertising and photography, manipulating them pictorially and grouping them in series alluding to man's place in a mass, highly-technological society. In his painting of the 80s, he turned towards abstraction.

Carlos Alcolea, Alfonso Fraile and Darío Villalba (Room 39) belong to that field of figurative art which burst upon the Spanish scene in the late 60s and early 70s. Alcolea's work belongs to the area of figurative narration, while that of Fraile, which went through several periods of abstraction, developed in the 70s into a peculiar form of figurative art full of strange characters composed of calligraphic lines. From his earliest works, Darío Villalba experimented with the photographic image, manipulating it pictorially with delicate transparencies.

EQUIPO CRÓNICA

Rafael Solbes y Manuel
Valdés

*Rafael Solbes was born in
Valencia in 1940, and died
there in 1981. Manuel Valdés
was also born in Valencia, in
1942. Formed by these two
painters,* Equipo Crónica
*made its appearance in the
provincial capital on the
River Turia in 1964,
although initially they were
joined by Juan Antonio
Toledo. The path taken by the
group developed within the
context of the movement
known as* Crónica de la
realidad, *which appeared in
the late 60s. Their images
have much in common with
European Pop Art, although
they are impregnated with
deep political and social
content.*

56

Equipo Crónica
Pintar es como golpear, 1972
(Painting is like Hitting)
Acrylic on canvas
152 x 202 cm
Reg. n° 12089

Several of the features typical of *Equipo Crónica's* work
have been commented on by Valeriano Bozal in the
following way: (...) "Some of *Equipo Crónica's* first paintings
allude directly to typically Spanish events, characters and
traditions, from parades to high society weddings, from an
official inauguration to the Spanish Parliament. On other
occasions, they include images from American mass
culture, which had taken root in Spain. In all cases they see
the image as a sign in a meaningful sequence, neither
emphasising, giving preference to nor glorifying any
particular one. The *Equipo* use a system of optical distortion
which preserves the objective parts of the image and avoids
the inclusion of direct personal features. They use acrylic
paint and often fall back on chipboard as a support as it
provides a clear surface. The dramatic character of their
work has given way to irony and sarcasm."

57

Eduardo Arroyo
*Toda la ciudad habla de
ello. El gato negro,* 1982
*(It's the Talk of the Town,
The Black Cat)*
Oil on canvas
162 x 162 cm
Reg. n° 08712

A R R O Y O

Eduardo ARROYO

*Born in Madrid in 1937. In
1958, one year after
completing his studies in
journalism in Madrid, he
moved to Paris, where
through his association with
the Spanish exiles who lived
there, his opposition to the
Franco regime became
reaffirmed. Almost at the
same time he began to paint,
exhibiting with the
L'Abattoir group in 1963.
Author of a number of
publications as well as a
painter and sculptor, Arroyo
is considered one of the main
representatives of Spanish Pop
Art, deeply and at times
ironically criticising political,
social and cultural systems
through his work.*

Francisco Calvo Serraller made the following observations
on Arroyo's night paintings: "From his views of the city
night which are the heart of the *Toda la ciudad habla de ello*
series, to his explicit, direct tribute to Francis Picabia's
Noche española ('Spanish Night'), Eduardo Arroyo not only
takes advantage of every opportunity to include the night as
the theme of his pictures, but he also turns his own
paintings into a battle of shadows. The subject is a delicate
one which demands close attention and eyes wide open, as
when one circumnavigates the night and all cats are black.
"The first thing to bear in mind where Arroyo's night is
concerned is that we should not fall into the trap of
concentrating on the anecdotal side of the picture only,
although everyone knows that Arroyo is a painter who has
raised the anecdotal to the level of a basic artistic principle.
All in all, the nocturnal side of the many ways in which
Eduardo Arroyo has depicted the night are a chapter apart –
the prologue to a novel in which there will later be a host of
shadows of greater or lesser brilliance, and stories lit by
street lamps. The nocturnal side of Arroyo's nights lies in
seeing everything in black."

GORDILLO

Luis Rodríguez Gordillo

*Born in Seville, in 1934.
After a stay in Paris, he
returned to Spain,
undergoing psychoanalysis in
1963, an experience which, as
he himself admitted, made a
deep impression on him and
was to act as a spur to his
pictorial work. In 1967, he
joined the* Nueva
Generación *group.
Beginning with abstract art,
his work drew gradually
closer to figurativeness, and
later even bordered on Pop
Art, although always from
Rodríguez's personal, critical
and ironic point of view. His
current works again tend
towards a personal kind of
abstraction.*

Luis Gordillo
Caballero cubista con lágrimas, 1973
(Cubist Gentleman with Tears)
Acrylic on canvas
160 x 106 cm
Reg. n° 11388

Francisco Calvo Serraller made the following observations
on Luis Gordillo's early 70s work: (...) "The build-up of
waste products was reaching incredible limits: informalist
automatism, figurative narration, pure colour contrasts,
shades of colour, deep perspective, plastic objectivism all
came together there... Which, translated into terms of
styles, meant the unification of all that was Expressionist,
Cubist, Surrealist, informalist, Pop and Constructivist...
This explosive cocktail was experienced in its most radical
phase by Gordillo until around 1973, after which time the
tension between figure and background began to ease,
meaning that colour no longer hindered the drawing so
acutely. (...)"

*T*he development of contemporary art from the 60s to the 80s
was so dynamic and diverse that many of the tendencies which
emerged intent on controversy soon became no more than traditional
movements. Art themes also changed notably. The spatial relationships
produced by the work and their effect on the spectator were methods
which conveyed a pragmatic conception of the art object rather than a
contemplative one. Such a process called into question the traditional
meaning of the museum – at times even questioning its very existence –
and made the creation of new kinds of exhibition spaces necessary.
The aim of Minimal Art, otherwise known as ABC-Art or the art of primary
forms, was to create visual forms reduced to a minimum – hence the
movement's name – as far as perception, form and semantics were concerned.
Its three-dimensional works lack any kind of argument or message and belong
to a particular type of abstract art of very basic structures, such as the cube
and the rectangular prism. Based on manufactured products, the works were
not usually made by the artist himself but by industrial companies, although
it was the former who provided the original sketches.
The first Minimalists – Carl André, Dan Flavin, Donald Judd, Sol le Witt and
Robert Morris – were active in New York between 1964 and 1968. They all
took part in major group exhibitions whose impact during this time was
enormous.
A precursor of Minimal Art, Barnett Newman (Room 40) at first took some of
the geometrical figures used by the European avant-garde between the wars as
his source of inspiration. However, he soon rejected all external influences and
created a style, or rather an idiom, of his own.
This room also contains a piece by Dan Flavin, who concentrated on the
modification of space through light. His illuminated areas thus become
sculptures which surround the spectator and momentarily change his time-
space coordinates.

Room 41 contains a work by Donald Judd, who concentrated on small forms, industrial construction, colour, research into the effects of scale, and, in his series, the use of arithmetic and geometric progression.

The work of another American, Bruce Nauman (Room 41), is also closely associated with Minimal Art. Here the spectator actually becomes part of the work, with a continuum in the work-artist-viewer relationship set up.

Rooms 40 and 41 contain pictures by Ellsworth Kelly, whose first works, despite signs of strong influence by Georges Vantongerloo, one of the founders of Dutch Neo-Plasticism, are directly inspired by forms in nature.

In his paintings, Robert Mangold (Room 41), whose work reflects the influence of artists such as Barnett Newman and Frank Stella, attempts to merge process and concept and to equate all the components of the picture – elements, lines, colours...

Pablo Palazuelo (Room 42) is a key figure of the Spanish Constructivist tendency. Although he is considered an adherent of geometric abstraction, his pictures reflect a highly personal style and are endowed with a profound sense of poetry. Palazuelo's three-dimensional pieces are always well-finished and rigorous in their conception of form.

Venezuela's Jesús Rafael Soto researches optical vibration and movement – both real and virtual – as applied to the work of art. The result of his research are works in which the general appearance of the exhibit changes as the observer moves around it in accordance with the principles of what is known as "virtual movement".

Next to Soto's exhibit there are works by two Spanish women painters – Elena Asíns and Soledad Sevilla (Room 43). Although the starting point of both these artists was geometric abstraction, the results were very different.

Room 44 brings together a number of pieces by the Zaj group, which was formed in 1964. Their approach has always included a keenly critical sense. Like Dada in its time, their notion of art subverted the conventional logic of representation and the relationship between the work and the spectator.

KELLY

Ellsworth Kelly

Born in Newburgh, New York, in 1923. In 1948, he travelled to Paris, staying there until 1954. The portraits he painted during the first months of his stay reflect the influence of Picasso, Byzantine art and Roman art, styles which had interested him since his years as a student in the United States. Not only a painter, he has also produced sculptures and reliefs, and has been described as one of the most genuine followers of Mondrian's Neo-Plasticism. Although he developed a form of representation to a certain extent close to geometric abstraction, his compositions with large octagonal planes and vibrant colour were often inspired by organic forms.

59

Ellsworth Kelly
Concorde, 1958
(Concorde)
Oil on canvas
193 x 147 cm.
Reg. n° 11487

Michel Seuphor, a friend of Kelly's, poetically described the work of this American artist who for some time lived in Paris in the following way: (...) "And here we have the American Kelly, who makes rhythmic surfaces whose style possesses even-tempered confidence and royal distinction. His virtuosity is surprising due to the very soberness of his media. Here even now we can see that, as with Palazuelo, Mondrian's patient lesson has borne fruit. Fruit which, let it be understood, has its own particular flavour. Kelly's art is as transparent and light as the morning air of mountain peaks. I would like to see it decorating airports inundated with light. His simple, delicately composed planes would be like sweet music helping the spirit to rise up to the lofty summits of imaginable perfection where all is calmness."

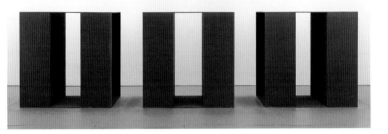

JUDD

Donald Judd

Born in Excelsior Spring, Missouri, U.S.A., in 1928, he died in New York in 1994. He attended the Art Students League in New York from 1948 to 1953, at the same time taking a degree in philosophy at the University of Columbia, where he graduated in 1953. He also graduated in history of art at Colombia in 1962. An art critic as well as a painter, his most important articles deal with Minimal Art, a tendency which he was one of the first to practise. Part of his work, which is of extraordinary formal consistency, has been on permanent display since 1986 at the Chinati Foundation in Marfa, Texas.

60

Donald Judd
***Untitled*, 1992**
Steel sheet
150 x 550 x 140 cm.
Reg. n° 11915

In 1965, in *Specific Objects* Donald Judd wrote of a new concept of Minimalist work beyond the ideas of painting and sculpture. Basically three-dimensional, the new works are unique in form and use industrial materials: "The three dimensions are real space. Which eliminates the problem of illusionism and literal space, of the space that surrounds or is contained in signs and colours (...) the numerous limitations of painting vanish. A work can be as strong as you want it to be. Real space is intrinsically more powerful, more specific than pigment on a flat surface (...). In three-dimensional works the overall object is built according to complex projects that are asserted in a single form. It is not necessary for a work to have a large number of forms to be considered, compared, analyzed or observed in turns. What is interesting is the work as a whole, its overall quality. Isolated essential things are more intense, more obvious, stronger (...). In the new works, form, image, colour and surface are united, they are not partial or dissociated."

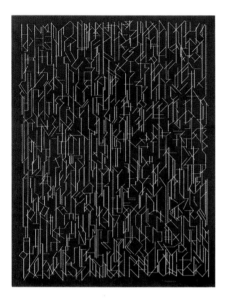

61

Pablo Palazuelo
Nigredo I, 1991
(Nigredo I)
Oil on canvas
170 x 133 cm.
Reg. n° DE-0259

In a text entitled "An Heir to Rimbaud", Yves Bonnefoy
made the following observations on Palazuelo: (...)
"Palazuelo's strokes have something of spiritual tension
about them, of walking almost in the open, beyond any
external image, which characterise certain mystics
(Spaniards like him, furthermore – St John of the Cross, for
example) and also teachers of Tantric painting or Muslim
calligraphy. And to my mind this newcomer to 'great art'
must be listened to carefully by all those who seek
transcendental conciseness in signs and a form of writing
which would be 'being'. For he has given others, whether
they have dreamt of a new language or a transformed
awareness or not, the dawning experience of a memory that
awakes, of an instant of premonition – the desire for and
even the reality of a new form of beauty."

SOTO

Jesús Rafael Soto

Born in Ciudad Bolívar,
Venezuela, in 1923. In 1950,
he moved to Paris, where he
joined the group of artists
associated with the Salon
des Réalités Nouvelles
and the Denise René
Gallery. *In 1953, he*
produced his
Desplazamiento
("Displacement") series,
which he complemented with
another known as Espiral
("Spiral") in 1955, both
precursors of kinetic art,
which was to be his style in
the future. In the early 60s,
he associated with the artists
of the Nouvelle Tendence
and the Zero *group, and*
took part with them in
group exhibitions. His first
works were inspired by the
geometric abstraction of
Malevich *and* Mondrian,
although he later turned to
optical vibrations and finally
produced his most personal
works of kinetic art.

62
....
Jesús Rafael Soto
Extensión amarilla y blanca, 1979
(Yellow and White Expanse)
Wood and painted metal
50 x 300 x 900 cm.
Reg. n° 07478

Vladimir Tismaneanu wrote on spectator participation in
Soto's works: "Soto's aesthetic dream is the construction
of an encompassing space, the result of strict control over
the elements of which it is composed, a space in which the
spectator actually becomes a part of the object's dynamism
in a reciprocal decision relationship. In this way, the rigid
demarcation of the sequences that make up the action of
aesthetic contemplation is excluded. More than that, Soto's
concept surpasses the contemplative, finally passive,
relationship, in favour of a dynamic, active connection in
which the work and the spectator become a single
configuration and communicate and merge."

ZAJ

Juan Hidalgo,
Walter Marchetti,
Esther Ferrer y
José Luis Castillejo

*Juan Hidalgo was born in
Las Palmas de Gran
Canaria in 1927, Walter
Marchetti in Italy, in 1931,
Esther Ferrer in San
Sebastián, in 1937, and José
Luis Castillejo in Seville, in
1932. They formed a group
in 1964. Their approach was
to combine the experimental
with the conceptual mainly
through their so-called*
Concerts, *adopting a critical
and provocative attitude to
society. As a group,* Zaj
*worked together until 1973.
Although the group has not
dissolved formally, since this
time each member has
followed his/her own artistic
course and has exhibited
individually.*

63 ....
Grupo Zaj
Cartones, 1969-70
(Cards)
Mixed media on paper

José Antonio Sarmiento made the following observations on
Zaj's cards and the events to which they refer: "Defined by
José Luis Castillejo as 'signs of existence', Zaj's *Cartones*
are carefully presented cards which offer those who receive
them a wide variety of proposals. Between 1964 and 1970,
texts, invitations to a concert in the home, poems,
greetings, calendars, crosswords, exhibitions, invitations,
etc., reached their addressees by mail and became one of
the most attractive and interesting ideas in mail-art whether
at home or abroad (...) Zaj concerts are a succession of
short actions or 'etceteras', as Juan Hidalgo called them,
that have nothing to do with the traditional concert (...) A
Zaj concert is, first and foremost, a visual spectacle and a
dramatization of everyday life in which Zen thought and the
Zaj family are present – i.e. Duchamp (the grandfather),
Cage (the father), Satie (the friend) and Durruti (the friend
of the friends), to whom we must add Marinetti (the
forgotten friend)."

*T*his room is intended as a temporary area for the Permanent Collection where holdings that have recently come into the Museum's possession or for any other reason are not permanently on display on Floor Four, will be exhibited for six to nine months. Furthermore, holdings belonging to other sources but connected in some way with the Museum Collections will also be exhibited temporarily in this room.

MOVEMENTS

SCHOOLS

GROUPS AND

TENDENCIES

GLOSSARY

Picasso in the La Californie Villa, Blue
Coast (France). Photograph by David
Douglas Duncan.

(*) The terms included refer to those used in the section dedicated to the **Permanent Collection**. In these, the English translation has been used when the term has been accepted as valid in English. Otherwise, the word is included in the original language.

Abstract Art. A tendency not based on the likeness of the motif represented by the visual image but on the arrangement of colours and forms, leaving the artist free to convey his feelings and experiences.

Abstract Expressionism. A term coined in 1929 by the American critic and historian Alfred H. Barr at first to describe Kandinsky's *Improvisations* and later (1946) the work of the post-war American artists who practised a type of abstract art in which great importance was attached to the gesture (the physical act of painting). These artists painted on canvases much larger than were usual at the time, covering the whole surface with pigment, which led to the term *All-over Field* (a composition in which the whole surface of the cloth is uniformly covered). The direct successor to Surrealist Automatism, this tendency is also known as Action Painting or the New York School.

Academia Breve de la Crítica de Arte. A group formed in 1941 by Eugenio D'Ors, whose aim as described in its *Proclama* was to disseminate in post-war Madrid "A few pages of contemporary universal art" and to organise future exhibitions to be called "Salones de los Once" at the *Biosca* Gallery in Madrid. Among the members of the *Academia Breve* were artists, architects, art critics, gallery owners, teachers and diplomats.

Action Painting. See **Abstract Expressionism**.

Art Autre ("Other Art"). A French expression which originated with a publication by the critic Michel Tapié in 1952. It was used to describe a type of art completely separate from other forms of expression. Its main exponents included painters such as Dubuffet, Fautrier, Mathieu and Wols. It is sometimes used as a synonym for informalism.

Art Povera ("Impoverished Art"). A term coined by the critic Germano Celant in 1967 to describe various exhibitions held in Italy at that time. It was very closely linked to Minimal Art as its exponents concentrated on the actual process of execution more than the finished work itself. They also used non-industrial, "poor" and at times unusual materials, such as grass, ice, sand, rubber, fat and even steam. Its adherents included Joseph Beuys, Jannis Kounellis, Mario Merz and Eva Hesse. It is also known as "Process Art".

Cobra. A group formed in 1948 by the painters Asger Jorn, Karel Appel, Constant, Corneille and the critics Christian Dotremont and Joseph Noiret. The name comes from the initials of the founder members' cities of origin: Copenhagen, Brussels and Amsterdam. In 1949, the painter Pierre Alechinsky joined them. The group worked together at the Marais workshops in Marais Street, Brussels. Influenced ideologically by Surrealism, their work can be described as an expressionist kind of figurative art close to the theories of American Action Painting. From the time the group was formed, their work received the support of the Stedelijk Museum in Amsterdam. In 1951, the members dispersed, although each continued to work individually along lines similar to those of the *Cobra* period.

Constructive Abstract Art. See **Constructivism**.

Constructivism. An abstract movement which appeared in Russia around 1913 and was led by Vladimir Tatlin, who upheld the supremacy of the construction over the representation and functionality of the work of art in accordance with social needs. Inspired by Cubism, the members of this movement produced a number of geometric compositions which subsequently influenced both painting and industrial design. Its influence extended to most geometric painting and the term "Constructivism" was even used to describe a number of movements which appeared in the 50s and 60s.

Crónica de la realidad. A figurative art movement which responded to the call to replace the apolitical standpoint of the figurative tendencies of the late 1950s with another, more critical, approach to social problems. Its subjects were usually violence, terror, the demythologization of historical and cultural events and a simple reflection of individual or group alienation. In Spain, its exponents included *Equipo Crónica* and Juan Genovés.

Cubism. An art movement which appeared around 1907 and whose central figures were Pablo Picasso and Georges Braque. Its aim was to represent volume by means of coloured surfaces, reducing nature to basic geometrical shapes and representing objects through their constant formal qualities. The immediate forerunner of Cubism was the late work of the French painter

Paul Cézanne. The movement went through three basic phases: *Analytical* Cubism (1908-1911), in which the object represented was submitted to a thorough analysis; *Hermetic* Cubism (1911), which inclined strongly towards abstraction; and *Synthetic* Cubism (1912-1914), in which iconographic selection was introduced to make the motif clearer. Cubism was to become one of the most important movements of the 20th century and it led to a large number of subsequent tendencies in art.

Dada. An art movement which appeared as an intellectual standpoint in 1916 under the leadership of the Romanian Tristan Tzara. Its members included painters, sculptors and poets from various parts of Europe who reacted against the absurdity and barbarity of World War I by rejecting established values in art and in other aspects of life. The form of freedom they upheld prompted them to choose new art processes such as the *ready-made* and the *collage*. The movement's name – Dada – was chosen by the founder by opening a dictionary at random, thus stressing the Dada philosophy of responding to the absurd within society with a personal sense of the absurd.

Dadaism. See **Dada**.

Dau al Set. A group which appeared in Barcelona in

1948 and was centred around the publication of the same name. It was formed by a number of artists and intellectuals, including Joan Brossa, Arnau Puig, Antoni Tàpies, Modest Cuixart, Joan Josep Tharrats and Joan Ponç. Inspired by Surrealism and Dada, *Dau al Set* was one of the most outstanding avant-garde groups in Spain after the Civil War.

De Stijl Movement. See **Neo-Plasticism**.

Expressionism. A tendency in which the expression of the artist's inner experiences prevails over the representation of the external world. In the field of painting and the plastic arts it is currently used to describe a specific art movement which developed at the beginning of the 20th century particularly in Germany and revolved around two groups, *Die Brücke* ("The Bridge", 1905-1913) and *Der blaue Reiter* ("The Blue Rider"), which appeared in 1911. In 1918, a third German Expressionist group appeared in the form of the *Neue Sachlichkeit* ("New Objectivity").

Fauvism. A pictorial movement which appeared in Paris in 1905 under Henri Matisse and brought together a number of painters including Derain, Vlaminck and Van Dongen, whom the critic Louis Vauxcelles dubbed *Les fauves* ("The Wild Beasts"). The movement is characterised by its free use of colour, the violence of its brush-strokes and the fact that its artists did not depict the external world in their works but their own feelings and psychological experiences.

Figurative Art. A form of art which, as opposed to abstract art, depicts identifiable visual images.

First School of Vallecas. See **School of Vallecas**.

Geometric(al) Abstraction. A form of abstract art in which, as opposed to Lyrical or Expressive Abstraction, lines, geometrical figures and, in most cases, plain colours predominate.

Geometric(al) Art. See **Geometric(al) Abstraction**.

Indaliano Movement. See **Indalianos**.

Indalianos. A group of painters from Almería led by Jesús de Perceval who held their first exhibition in 1946. They advocated a new form of aesthetics inspired by classical and surrealist elements and related to the Algar culture and the campaniform vessel. Its members were Capuleto, Luis Cañadas, Francisco Alcaraz, Antonio López Díaz and Miguel Cantón Checa.

Informal Art. See **Informalism**.

Informalism. An abstract tendency which appeared with the outbreak of World

War II in France partly as a reaction to American Abstract Expressionism. It is characterised by a total absence of formal structure, excluding even geometrical forms or any interest in the blot, matter, texture or calligraphic outline as direct expressions of the painter's own ego. Informalism came to Spain basically through Antoni Tàpies (Barcelona) and the *El Paso* group (Madrid).

Kinetic Art. A tendency which appeared in the mid-60s and includes all works incorporating movement, whether real or virtual. Kinetic Art appeared as the direct result of the *Realist Manifesto* issued by Pevsner and Gabo in 1920, and there are three basic types: those works which have real movement produced by small motors; the "transformables", whereby it is the spectator himself who moves or manipulates the work; and the static works, which have no real movement but are capable of producing optical effects through optical illusion. This last form is also known as *Op Art* or *Optical Art*.

LADAC. ("The Archers of Contemporary Art"). A group of Canarian artists who formed around its theoretician, Edward Westerdahl. They made their first public appearance at the *Syra* Gallery in Barcelona in 1951. Among LADAC's members were Felo Monzón, Juan Ismael, José Julio and Manuel Millares, all of whose works combined

respect for the autochthonous Canarian culture with the teachings of the international avant-garde.

Los Arqueros del Arte Contemporáneo. See **LADAC**.

Magic Realism. See **Neue Sachlichkeit**.

Minimal Art. A term coined in 1965 by the philosopher Richard Wollheim in reference to works of art which turned away from traditional painting or sculpture. It was immediately applied to a new current in the United States which had appeared as a reaction to *Pop Art* and grouped together several tendencies whose aim was to create visual forms reduced to the minimum vis-à-vis perception and structure. Works of this type are composed of extremely simple geometrical structures – lines, cubes, neon tubes. Minimal Art's best-known exponents are Dan Flavin, Carl André, Sol Le Witt, Robert Morris and Donald Judd. It is also known as "ABC Art" and the "Art of Primary Structures".

Modernisme. An art style found in a number of countries at the turn of the century which mainly influenced architecture and the decorative arts. It is characterised by a predilection for decoration and ornamentation, although structural functionality was always given priority. Lines, arabesques and plant forms play a prominent part in its iconographic repertoire. *Modernisme's* importance lies in its having attempted to do away with the traditional differences between the "fine arts" (painting, sculpture and architecture) and the "minor arts" (engraving, drawing and the "sumptuous" or applied arts). Its name varies according to each country, examples being *Art Nouveau, Stile Liberty, Sezessionisti, Jugendstil* and *Modern Style.*

Neo-Plasticism. A Dutch movement which appeared in 1917 at the same time as its organ, the magazine *De Stijl*, and which was endorsed by the painter Piet Mondrian. Inspired by Cubism, Neo-Plasticism advocated the use of the right angle only and no more than six colours: the three primaries – blue, red and yellow – and the three "non-colours" – black, white and grey. The movement's influence extended to other fields beyond the pictorial, especially to architecture, sculpture and industrial design.

Neue Sachlichkeit ("New Objectivity"). A realism-based movement which appeared in Germany around 1925 and whose members included artists such as Grosz, Otto Dix, Karl Hubbuch, Rudolf Schlichter, Anton Räderscheidt, Carl Grossberg and Christian Schad. Convinced of the social function of art, its followers bitterly criticised the social mores of the Germany of the 1920s. The movement in fact consisted of two groups, that known as the *Neue Sachlichkeit*, a term encompassing the whole movement and characterised by its more radical ideas, and *Magic Realism*, a faction closer to Surrealism which took its name from the book of the same title by Franz Roh published in 1925.

New Objectivity. See **Neue Sachlichkeit.**

New York School. See **Abstract Expressionism.**

Noucentisme. A Catalan term meaning literally "1900-ism" and used in reference to a Catalan movement of between 1906 and 1931 whose central figure was Eugenio D'Ors. It appeared as a reaction to *Modernisme* and proposed a return to classicism and order in art. Its main exponents were Josep Clará, Enric Casanovas and Joaquim Sunyer.

Optical Art. See **Kinetic Art.**

Optical Kinetic Art. See **Kinetic Art.**

Orphism. A term coined by Guillaume Apollinaire in 1912 to describe Robert Delaunay's work. This movement coincided with Cubism as far as form was concerned but unlike it included colour in its compositions and attached a great deal of importance to light, thus linking up to a certain extent with Impressionism. Other representatives of Orphism were Sonia Delaunay and Frantisek Kupka. Together with the works of Kandinsky, Robert Delaunay's Orphic works can be considered as the first examples of 20th-century abstract art. .

Other Art. See **Art Autre.**

Paris School. The name given to a number of mainly European artists who made the French capital their habitual place of work and residence, especially during the period after World War I and until the outbreak of World War II, at which point the avant-garde moved to New York. Of great importance to the emergence of a large number of subsequent art movements, its only common denominator was that its members lived in the city from which its name was taken.

Pop Art. A style which developed basically in the United States and Great Britain in the mid-50s. The term *Pop* was coined by the critic Lawrence Alloway and is used to describe art manifestations based on the popular culture that emerges in the urban areas of the most industrialized societies. *Pop* artists use realist figurativeness as a means of expression and through it depict an iconography taken from mass culture characterised by the use of images from the media. Its main exponents include: Robert Rauschenberg, Jasper Johns, Roy Lichtenstein, Andy Warhol, Claes Oldenburg, Tom Wesselmann, James Rosenquist, Richard Hamilton, Peter Blake, Richard Smith, David Hockney, Peter Phillips and Allen Jones.

Pórtico Group. An art group which appeared in Saragossa in 1947. Its main members were the painters Eloy Laguardia, Santiago Lagunas and Fermín Aguayo, who produced the first abstract compositions in the Spanish art of their times.

Realism. A term used to describe aesthetic attitudes or tendencies concerned with the faithful reproduction of reality. The artist's personal view of reality was sometimes included in the picture.

Salones de los Once. See **Academia Breve de la Crítica del Arte**.

School of Altamira. An art movement which appeared in 1948 and brought together a number of painters and critics led by the German artist Mathias Goeritz. With its cosmopolitan outlook it furthered cultural exchange between artists of the Spanish avant-garde and a number of leading international painters and sculptors.

School of Vallecas. A school developed in Madrid in 1927 by the painter Benjamín Palencia and the sculptor Alberto Sánchez, who were subsequently joined by other figures from the worlds of art and literature, including Juan Manuel Díaz Caneja, Maruja Mallo, José Bergamín, Rafael Alberti and Federico García Lorca. Their aim was to revitalize Spanish art by emulating the Paris experience. The name comes from the artists' choice of the Vallecas countryside as the central theme of their work. The group is also known as the *First School of Vallecas*.

Stijl, De. See **Neo-Plasticism**.

Surrealism. A literary and artistic movement which appeared in 1924 and was led by the writer and poet André Breton. With Sigmund Freud's discoveries in psychoanalysis as its starting point, its theories advocated free access to the images of the subconscious dispensing with the mediation of rational control by using the two basic processes which made up the Surrealist techniques par excellence – *Automatism* and *dépaysement réfléchi* ("reflexive disorientation"). The Surrealists also invented creative games,

such as the *exquisite corpse*. The movement produced two forms of representation – *objective line*, which imitated forms of reality, and *anti-objective line*, which was more or less abstract and did not reproduce natural forms.

Tachisme. A term from the French *tache* ("blot") first used around 1950 by the critic Michel Seuphor to describe an abstract pictorial trend in which great importance was attached to the improvised blot or stain of colour as a way of painting automatically. This trend was closely linked to American Abstract Expressionism and in particular to "Drip Painting". Its main exponents were Wols, Mathieu, Hartung and Saura.

Valori Plastici. ("Plastic Values"). An art movement which appeared in Rome in 1918 in association with the magazine of the same name. Its aim was to bring about what was known as a "return to order", i.e. to replace the avant-garde movements, especially Cubism and Expressionism, with a new type of art manifestation inspired by classical models. In 1922, the group changed its name to *Novecento*, taking up a more radical position and identifying itself with the nationalistic and fascist ideas then prevalent in Italy.

SELECTION OF AVANT-GARDE
MOVEMENTS AND GROUPS

This list contains only those movements regarded as historical

Name	Appeared	Principal representatives
Impressionism	1870	Monet, Degas, Renoir, Manet, Pisarro, Sisley
Symbolism	1880	Puvis de Chavannes, Moreau, Redon
Neo-Impressionism	1884	Seurat, Signac
Post-Impressionism	1886	Cézanne, Gauguin, Van Gogh, Toulouse Lautrec
Modernisme	1890	Horta, Guimard, Gallé, Mackintosh, Van de Velde, Hankar, Wagner, Olbrich, Gaudí
Fauvism	1905	Matisse, Derain, Vlaminck, Dufy, Braque, Roualt
Expressionism	1905	Nolde, Kirchner, Schmidt-Rottluff, Javlensky, Grosz, Dix
Cubism	1907	Picasso, Braque, Gris, Duchamp-Villon, Archipenko, Lipchitz, Zadkine
Futurism	1909	Boccioni, Balla, Carrà, Severini, Sant'Elia
Purism	1910	Le Corbusier, Ozenfant
Orphism	1912	Delaunay (Robert and Sonia), Kupka
Section d'Or	1912	Villon, Duchamp
Tubism or Machine Art	1912	Léger
Suprematism	1913	Malevich
Constructivism	1913	Tatlin, El Lissitzky, Pevsner, Gabo
Dada	1916	Janco, Arp, Duchamp, Picabia, Ernst, Schwitters, Hausmann
Metaphysical Painting	1917	Chirico, Carrà, Morandi, Campigli
Neo-Plasticism	1917	Mondrian, Van Doesburg, Rietveld, Vantongerloo
Bauhaus	1919	Gropius, Klee, Kandinsky, Moholy-Nagy, Albers
Surrealism	1924	Dalí, Magritte, Delvaux, Ernst, Tanguy, Masson, Miró, Giacometti
Abstract Expressionism	1946	Pollock, Kline, De Kooning, Motherwell
Informalism	1950	Mathieu, Fautrier, Michaux, Dubuffet

(*) The terms included refer to those used in the section dedicated to the **Permanent Collection**. In these, the English translation has been used when the term has been accepted as valid in English. Otherwise, the word is included in the original language.

Academicism. A term describing an artistic phenomenon characterised by the use of a set of rigid, uninspiring rules which impede free creativity. This term is also used in reference to works which faithfully reflect traditional subjects or forms but verge on the stereotype.

Arabesque. Decoration based on intertwining lines with a profusion of curves. Originally an Arabic technique, it was widely used by the exponents of *Modernisme*.

Assemblage. A French term describing a process deriving originally from collage in which a number of preferably industrial objects are used together in a work of art.

Automatism. A Surrealist method consisting of drawing or writing without logic, allowing the hand and the brush to move freely and without control. Used mainly in writing, painting and drawing, it subsequently gave rise to the technical and methodological basis of Action Painting, culminating in the "Drip Painting" automatic painting process.

Avant-garde. A term applied to the various innovative tendencies which

have appeared in the 20th century in the arts and literature.

Blot. After the French "tache". A pictorial medium used by the French abstract tendency known as *Tachisme* which consists of applying blobs of colour at random over the surface of the canvas and using these to paint haphazardly. It can be considered as a process related to Surrealist Automatism.

Bodegón. A Spanish pictorial genre whose subject is primarily still life (dead animals, flowers, fruit, etc.), although in the background there may be an interior, with or without figures. The term originated in the 18th century, although the genre itself is older.

Bronze. A tin and copper alloy. A work of art made of bronze.

Brush-stroke. A stroke made by the artist's brush to apply colour directly to the surface of the support.

Canvas. A cloth, especially of flax, cotton or hemp, used for painting on. A painting on canvas.

Classicism. A term describing all artistic manifestations, including

literature and music, inspired by Graeco-Roman art as an ideal.

Colour. The impression made on the retina by the rays of light reflected by an object. The three primary colours – blue, red and yellow – are the basis of all other colours, which are obtained by mixing the former. Colours are said to be pure when they are not mixed or reduced by the addition of black.

Collage. From the French "coller" meaning "to stick". A technique in which any type of material, although preferably paper, is pasted onto a support (canvas, cardboard, etc.). It was first used by Picasso and Braque in their Cubist works.

Composition. The arrangement or structure of the different elements, motifs, forms and colours which make up a work of art.

Constructive. See **Constructivism**.

Chipboard. A compact material made from wood splinters mixed with an agglutinating agent (glue, etc.) and pressed to give it consistency. It is suitable for use as a support for painting.

Drawing. A technique of graphic representation in which an image is made on a surface by means of implements such as pencils, pens, canes, etc. In most cases a single colour is used.

Drip Painting. A pictorial technique in which paint is poured onto the support (which is usually laid on the floor) along a rod puncturing the bottom of a tin of paint. This process was occasionally used by Max Ernst, although it was Jackson Pollock who popularised it within the context of Action Painting in 1947. Drip painting can be considered a direct result of Surrealist Automatism.

Execution. The carrying out, making of a work of art.

Exquisite Corpse. From the French "Cadavre exquis", a creative game of Surrealist origin in which each player writes down one word on a piece of paper without seeing what the others have previously written. The name of the game comes from the first sentence written through this process, "The exquisite corpse will drink the new wine."

Figure. The artistic representation of the human or animal form.

Forging. A way of working metal, particularly iron, by exposing it to fire in a forge and shaping it on an anvil with a hammer. By extension, working with wrought metal.

Form. The shape, external appearance given to a material. What is appreciated of the material by the senses or by examining the surface.

Format. The shape and size of a picture, drawing, etc. Usually expressed as vertical and horizontal, and small, medium and large formats.

Frottage. A French term meaning "rubbing". A technique which consists of rubbing a pencil or crayon over a piece of paper or a canvas placed on an irregular surface made of wood, cloth, etc. to obtain its relief design. It was a Surrealist process much used by Max Ernst.

Gestural painting. A general term used to describe the physical gestures used by an artist when painting. It is used particularly in connection with Action Painting.

Gouache. See **Wash**.

Graphite. A greyish-black mineral of almost pure carbon used for drawing.

Grisaille. From the French. A painting in grey or greyish monochrome. It was widely used in the 16th century.

Gypsum. Hydrated calcium sulphate. Dense or earthy, when it is dehydrated through heat and ground it can be used as a material for building and sculpting as it sets quickly when mixed with water.

Hollow. See **Void**.

Horror Vacui. A Latin term meaning literally "Horror of the void". It is used to describe compositions in which the various motifs completely fill the surface of the picture.

Iconic. Pertaining to an image.

Iconography. The identification and description of certain art themes which are mutually and specifically consistent, whether socially or intellectually. Iconography includes the study of the changes which such themes undergo with the passage of time and through contact with different cultural environments.

Impasto. Mixture of oil or tempera colours. The term has also come to be used to describe the effect obtained by applying this mixture to a support in different thicknesses.

Indian ink. A liquid originally made from lampblack, size and certain fragrant substances, such as camphor or musk. Used for drawing, it gives a permanent and uniform colour. The original manufacturing process has now been replaced by other industrial processes.

Installation. A term very much in fashion in the

GLOSSARY

1970s, particularly in the United States. It was used for works of art erected especially for the exhibition on the museum or gallery premises.

Maquette. A scale reproduction or sketch of a sculpture or a work of architecture.

Matter. In the language of art criticism a term applied to the material used for colouring, i.e. the pigment. More recently its meaning covers any material used in producing a work of art – paper, cloth, wood, plastic and, in general, waste materials of any kind.

Metamorphosis. A theme typical of Surrealism which corresponds to the mottoes governing the movement's ethic: "Change life" and "Transform the world".

Mixed media. A combination of various types of physical material used in a work of art.

Subject. The theme or motif dealt with in a work of art.

Mobile. A work of art which includes movement produced either by elements unconnected with it such as the air or the spectator, or by any kind of mechanical power.

Model. A figure or object reproduced by the artist in his work. Also a person who poses for a painter or sculptor. Also, to make figures or motifs with a

malleable substance such as clay, wax, etc.

Monochrome. Of a single colour, including all its possible tones.

Motif. The subject of a work of art.

Movement. A broader term than "style" used for the set of artistic or ideological manifestations with specific characteristics which endow it with unity and constitute a perceptible change with respect to previous manifestations.

Objet Trouvé. A French term meaning "Found object". An object of no value, found by chance by the artist, who uses it as part of a work of art or as a work in itself. It was first used in painting and the plastic arts by Dada's Kurt Schwitters.

Oil. A pictorial medium used from the 15th century onwards which consists of dissolving colours in an oily agglutinating agent, such as linseed, walnut or animal oil to which volatile substances such as turpentine are added to aid drying. Also, a picture painted with this technique.

Outline. The line which defines a figure, object or composition.

Painting. An art technique in which pigments or colours dissolved in a variety of substances are applied to a surface for representational, expressive or decorative

purposes. A pictorial work. What is represented in a pictorial work.

Palette knife. An implement usually of wood or metal used to apply colours and spread them over the picture.

Palette. A tray made of wood, metal, ceramic, glass, etc., on which the painter sets out his colours and mixes them. By extension, his choice of colour as seen in his work.

Paranoiac-critical method. From the French *Méthode paranoïaque-critique*. A research system devised by Salvador Dalí during his period with the Surrealist movement which caused a veritable revolution in the theoretical foundations of the movement.

Perspective. A method with which it is possible conventionally to represent objects in three dimensions on a surface.

Pictorial. Pertaining to the art of painting.

Pigment. Any substance which, when mixed with a liquid, becomes a coloured medium that can be used for painting. Pigments can be organic (of animal or plant origin) or inorganic (mineral), although both are now produced artificially.

Plane. In a picture, an imaginary surface determined by the objects depicted as situated at the same distance from the real surface of the picture.

Plaster. Calcined gypsum which is mixed with water and used as a material in sculpture, especially for making moulds.

Plasticity. The qualities of a work which make it expressive, especially with regard to the sensation of volume.

Plein air. A French term meaning "open air". It is used to describe pictures painted outside the artist's study without artificial lighting. "Open air" painting was common during the Impressionist period.

Plywood. A sheet of wood made of three or more veneers glued over each other at right angles.

Process. See **Technique**.

Ready-made. Used to describe a prefabricated or industrially produced object raised by the artist to the level of a work of art without changing its external appearance in any way. The term was first used by Marcel Duchamp.

Reflexive disorientation. From the French *Dépaysement réfléchi*. A Surrealist technique in which images from the subconscious are depicted by capturing mutually unconnected objects in perfectly logical spaces obtained through Renaissance perspective.

Relief. A piece of sculpture projecting from a flat surface. There are three types: "low relief", *mezzo rilievo* and "high relief".

Repoussé. From the French "pushed back". Metal hammered into a relief. This technique can also be used on leather by placing it over a piece of smooth plastic, wetting it and compressing parts of it in such a way that when it is dry these will stand out in relief.

Representation. The reproduction of the image or appearance of a thing.

Ronde-bosse. A sculpture in the round, as opposed to relief.

Rotten Donkey. From the French "Âne pourri". A theme from the iconography of Salvador Dalí's Surrealist works in which a rotting dead donkey was depicted. Putrefaction as a motif was to extend to all the types of matter – both organic and inorganic – featured in Dalí's canvases, particularly in those of 1929 and 1930.

Sculpture. Art in which solid materials are given three-dimensional form and represent the shape of an object, figure or motif whether real or imaginary. A work by a sculptor.

Sketch. A preliminary study of the work of art. Due to the spontaneity with which it is usually carried out, the sketch gives an interesting insight into the artist and his work.

Still life. A painting of inanimate objects.

Stroke. A line, strip or stroke made with a pencil or a paintbrush.

Structuring. See **Structure**.

Style. A series of original, constant characteristics of an artist, period, school or geographical area which enable individual or group works to be identified.

Structure. A general way of arranging elements in relation to one another in order to obtain a consistent and organic whole. A group of elements forming a structure.

Support. The surface on which the pictorial work is executed. Traditionally the materials most commonly used as supports are canvas, board and walls, but all kinds of materials are now used.

Technique. The procedures and resources used by an artist to carry out his/her work.

Tendency. A group of artistic ideas or processes leading in the same direction and pursuing the same aims. They are usually expressed or made public through manifestos or written programmes.

Terracotta. Clay used for making pottery and sculptures which is subsequently fired.

Texture. The structure of the material in a work of

art. It may give a bumpy, rough, smooth, shiny, velvety, etc., finish to the work.

Tone. The intensity or degree of brightness of a colour, whether alone or in relationship to the others on the surface of the work. There are several types – warm, cool and neutral.

Treatment. The process used in making a work of art.

Vanitas. A Latin term meaning "vanity". A form of still life often featuring skulls, clepsydrae and other objects alluding to the transience of life. These compositions also contain inscriptions stressing the fleeting nature of time, such as *Vanitas vanitatum*, from

which the name of this type of picture is taken. It was a common theme in the work of its leading 17th-century exponents, the Spanish artists Valdés Leal and Pereda.

Version. Any one of the representations of a subject or theme in art or music.

Void. A concavity or hollow in a three-dimensional work of art.

Volume. Mass, the amount of space occupied by an object.

Wash. From the French "gouache". A pictorial technique in which colour diluted in water is applied. It is different from watercolour in that lead

white is used, both for deeper shades and for lightening others, in order to make them more opaque.

Watercolour. A pictorial technique using transparent colours made with gum arabic dissolved in water. White is not used, being replaced by the colour of the paper, which is the usual support (although in China and Japan silk is also used).

Welding. The joining of one thing to another by fusing the material itself at the point of joining with a material of the same or similar kind. In oxyacetylene welding no other material is used, the surfaces of the two parts joined being welded to each other.

© ALDEASA ® 1997
Legal Deposit: M-24.715-97
ISBN: 84-8003-080-1

Design: Mar Lissón / Natalia Arranz
Cover: Talía Hormigo
Layout: Myriam López Consalvi
Photographs: MNCARS archives. Joaquín Cortés / José Municio
For authorised reproductions: © VEGAP, Madrid 1997, © DEMART PROARTE B.V.,
© FUNDACIÓ ANTONI TÀPIES, © FUNDACIÓ PILAR Y JOAN MIRÓ, © The Artists,
Madrid 1997
Photomechanical production: Lucam, Madrid
Translation: Nigel Williams
Front cover photo: *Mujer sentada acodada (Seated Woman Leaning on Her Elbows),*
by Pablo Picasso. 1939
Printed in Spain by: Estudios Gráficos Europeos

Printed in Spain